ALL ABOUT WICKER

ALL ABOUT

A Dutton Paperback

WICKER

patricia corbin

E. P. DUTTON | NEW YORK

CONTENTS

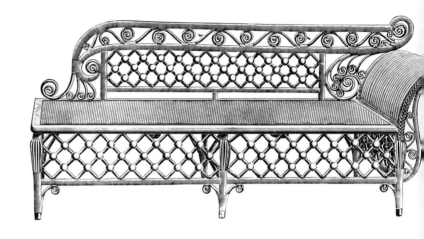

INTRODUCTION

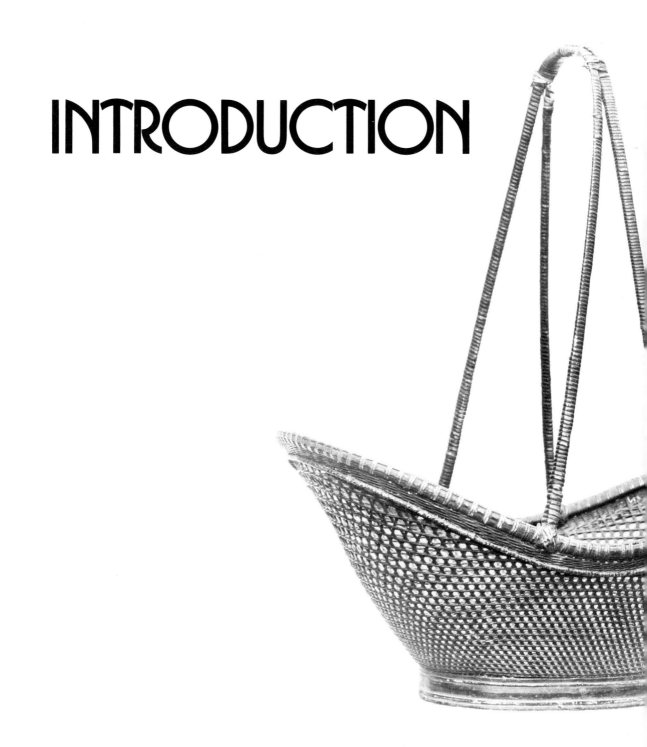

Wycre. Wykyr. Wykker. Wicker. Its spelling has changed over time, but its meaning hasn't. Wicker is something that's woven, mostly from rattan (which includes cane, pole, reed, and peel), but also from willow, straw, rush, raffia, palm, dried grasses, spun wood pulp (fiber), buri, or bamboo. There are headrests of wicker, floor mats, hats, shoes, tea strainers, spice containers, all manner of boxes and baskets—even houses and hearses. But the way we know wicker best, what we think of when we think wicker, is as furniture; and that's what this book is all about.

Wicker furniture has had its ins and outs in the history of home furnishings, but it was never so popular as in Victorian times. People were wild about wicker; they put it into every room in the house. They're doing it again today—probably for the same reasons: wicker is natural, handmade, comfortable. It is new and at the same time old; rustic, yet exotic; and although it may take the most simple or the most elaborate forms to reflect the taste of the times, it always maintains an integrity of its own.

Perhaps the oldest piece of wicker furniture known was a hassock, one that was coiled and woven into a round stool, a simple but elegant design shown in a sculpture from Syria (c. 2600 B.C.). Probably one of the finest pieces of ancient wicker still existing is a toilet chest from the burial site of Queen Menuthotep at Thebes (c. 1600 B.C.). The construction of the chest and the wrapping of the joints are akin to the methods used in making wicker furniture today. The tomb of King Tutankhamun (who died c. 1325 B.C.) included some finely woven wicker furniture—stools and chests—along with baskets, matting, and a pair of wicker sandals.

Wicker furniture from the Greek civilization is known only in stone carvings; but written accounts, as well as stone carvings, have survived from the Roman Empire that prove there were woven furnishings around the time of Christ. Willows were cultivated

Chinese headrest, early 20th century. This is a classic wicker design, hollow on the inside, woven of natural rattan in a twill weave, bordered in black. A household object since the Ming dynasty (c. 1400). More elaborate and sophisticated headrests were gilded and lacquered. H. 5″; L. 15½″; W. 5¼″. Courtesy Field Museum of Natural History, Chicago.

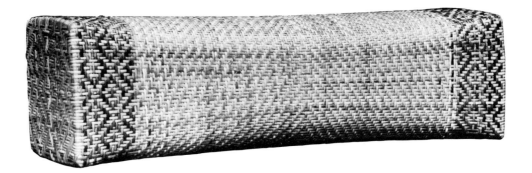

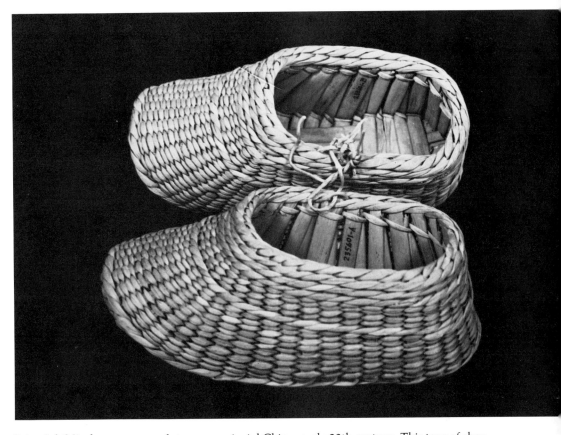

Pair of child's shoes, woven of straw, provincial China, early 20th century. This type of shoe is universal throughout China, with weaves and types of straw varying from province to province. The weaving of straw and bamboo has been an important Chinese craft since the Stone Age. These shoes were part of a folk art exhibition at China House Gallery, New York City, along with dozens of bamboo objects—wine pots and cosmetic boxes, and even a bamboo jacket worn in the 18th century as an undergarment for insulation. H. 2½"; L. 6½"; W. 2¾". Courtesy Field Museum of Natural History, Chicago.

Japanese rain suit. Probably before middle of 19th century. Straw on string netting, with wicker hat, leggings, and boots. Photograph from *Costumes of the East*, © 1971, The American Museum of Natural History, New York.

Bamboo flower basket from Wenchou, Chechiang, China, early 19th century. The weaving pattern is centuries old, a traditional open, twined, and coiled technique using threadlike bamboo strips. Even though the shape is a simple boat, there are traces of gold paint on the base and rim. H. 8½" (without handle); L. 14"; W. 10½". Courtesy Field Museum of Natural History, Chicago.

This double-tier oval box shows a charming handcraft painstakingly made, dated and signed. It is composed of two compartments with five layers of twilled weaving alternating with very delicate bamboo strips, smaller and finer than split matchsticks. The Chinese characters down the middle of the handle read "Made with pure heart by Madame Ku of Linen in 1888." H. 11"; W. 11". Courtesy Field Museum of Natural History, Chicago.

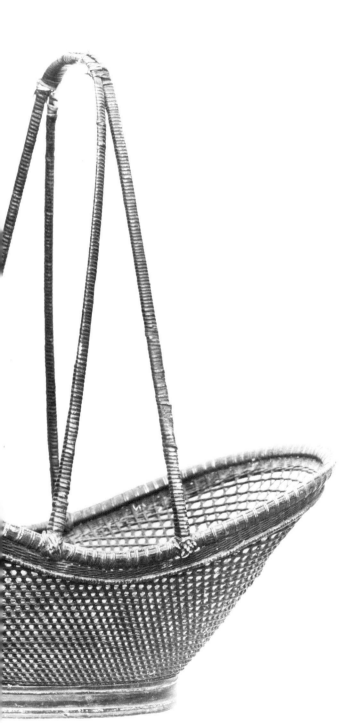

A rectangular basket shows the intricate hexagonal weave indigenous to the Fuchien province, China, early 19th century. Three strips of bamboo beginning at the wooden base run up the sides to shape the handle, around which additional strips of bamboo are coiled, making an extremely sturdy carryall. H. 12″; W. 7″. Courtesy Field Museum of Natural History, Chicago.

in Rome for weaving agricultural tools, utensils, chariot carts, and various designs of furniture. Pliny, in his *Natural History* (bk. 16, chap. 68), spoke of the whiter willow being "particularly useful in the construction of those articles of luxury, reclining chairs." A stone relief carving (early third century) near Treves, West Germany, shows a Roman woman sitting in a basket chair very much like those made today.

The Britons inherited the basket chair from the Romans. Its low price and modest appearance made it the common people's chair throughout the Middle Ages. The

basket chair was sometimes called the "twiggen" or "beehive" chair. A basketworker was known as a "twiggy"; twiggen was a synonym for wicker. "I'll beat the knave into a wicker bottle," Cassio threatens (*Othello*, Act II, scene 2), but Shakespeare first wrote "twiggen bottle." In his third edition of *Sylvia* (1679), John Evelyn recommends the use of the many varieties of willow for "boxes such as apothecaries and goldsmiths use," and the osiers of willow for "all wicker and twiggie works, particularly for the construction of chairs."

Wicker hearse, early 1900s, Funchal, Madeira Island, has a double sedan chair (meant to seat two) with rolled back, wide braid trim, and tufted upholstery. It is remarkably like popular contemporary wicker chairs designed by Peter Rocchia of Wickerworks. Courtesy Mrs. John G. Winslow.

These Iraqi marsh dwellers weave their extraordinary houses from the six- to ten-meters-long reeds that grow all around them. The intricate constructions display considerable technical virtuosity. Courtesy Société Française de Promotion Artistique, Paris.

Seventeenth-century paintings by the Flemish artist Jacob Jordaens show two styles of tightly woven wicker chairs. One was similar to a sixteenth-century French wicker chair called a "guérite," meaning sentry box. It had deep wings that formed an arched canopy to ward off drafts inside, and to protect from the sunlight outside. Chairs of similar design were listed as early as 1571 in English farm inventories. The other chair Jordaens painted resembled the classic wing chair of the eighteenth century, with a high, squared-off back, side panels, and armrests.

Wicker came to America on the *Mayflower*, as a cradle for a baby named Peregrine White. Chairs of wicker, probably basket chairs, were made by early Colonists; but the industry was small. There was neither the raw material to support a larger one, nor the demand: wicker was not an especially important part of Colonial home decoration.

But then came the China trade. By the time the English took the lead from the Dutch, in the mid-1700s, the only Chinese port open to foreigners was Canton. It was in Canton, in the gardens of wealthy merchants, that American and British traders saw their first peacock chairs. According to legend, the mandarins had used the chair as a sort of throne, and often jewels were woven into the fantail backrest to create the iridescent illusion of peacock feathers. Peacock chairs were among the many Oriental articles imported by this country at that time. Yankee clipper ships brought their exotic cargoes home, protected by dunnage of rattan. The dunnage was discarded on the docks for almost a hundred years before a grocer named Cyrus Wakefield picked up a bundle and brought it home. He thought he might try fixing an old rocking chair with it. Ten years later he was designing the wicker chairs that his company would weave from the rattan that he had begun to import. Wicker was on its way to becoming a major American industry and the darling of Victorian society.

This sweet-faced-looking little man with the patrician nose (a sculpture owned by the Louvre) was a kitchen servant in Syria c. 2600 B.C. He is wearing a wicker skirt of palm fronds and sitting on the oldest piece of woven furniture known to man—a wicker hassock. Courtesy Union des Musées Nationaux, Paris.

Egyptian toilet chest, 17th Dynasty. c. 1600
B.C. Woven of reed and papyrus with strutted
framework. Furniture made from papyrus
and other fibers antedated carpentry and continued
throughout dynastic times. As furnishings in
even the most prosperous houses were sparse, a
chest of this type was an important and functional
piece, meant to hold jewelry, wigs, and toilet
requisites. Courtesy Staatliche Museen zu
Berlin/DDR, Ägyptisches Museum.

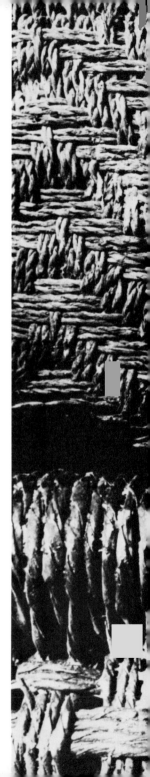

Woven rush fragments, First Dynasty, typical
of the weaving in light stools used in Egyptian homes.
The wide range of weaving was abundantly seen in
King Tutankhamun's tomb—everything from everyday
objects and furnishings to a toy slingshot, and even a
pair of fancy gauntlet-type gloves. Courtesy
Robert Harding Associates, London.

A chair, carved to simulate cane-wrapped bamboo and decorative woven rattan (see detail) made for Marie-Antoinette in 1787 by Georges Jacob for her trellised bedroom at the Petit Trianon, Versailles. Discovered at Château-sur-Mer, the Wetmore mansion in Newport, Rhode Island, and auctioned at Parke-Bernet in New York for $4,500 in the 1960s. Courtesy J. Paul Getty Museum, Malibu, California.

This wicker cradle was brought over on the *Mayflower*. It was possibly made in Holland, or in the Far East. Courtesy Pilgrim Hall Museum, Plymouth.

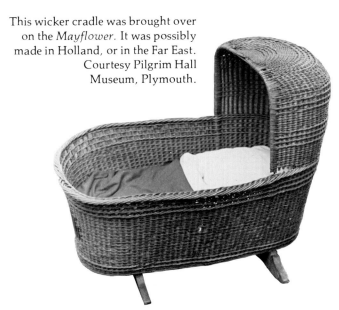

VICTORIAN

WICKER

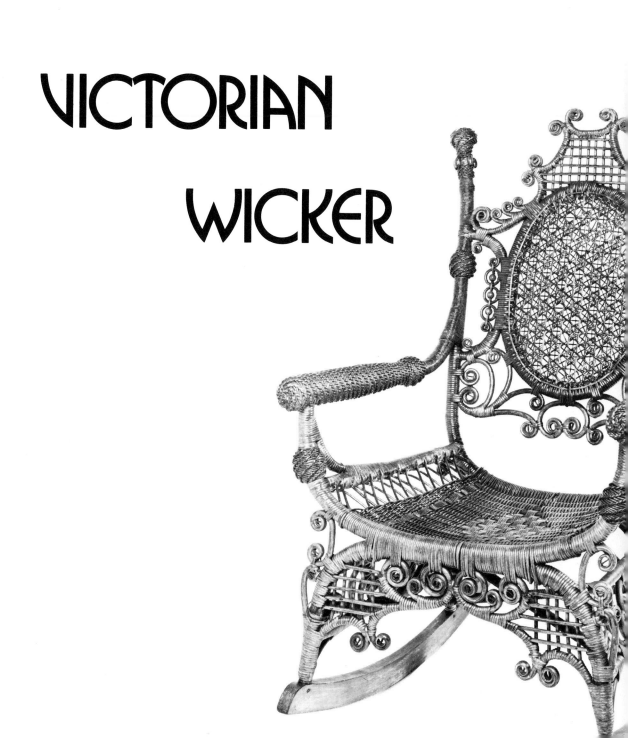

The Victorians, for all their primness and propriety, were not prim and proper consumers. They were passionate ones. Their world bustled with industry and commerce, offering them a wealth of goods, newly manufactured at home, newly imported from abroad—a temptation of luxuries and marvels in which they heartily indulged. Their homes bulged with the treasure.

Home was an ideal, the place where the Victorians expected to find their pleasure in life, and it seems they found an almost sensuous pleasure decorating it. With loving abandon they filled each room with a bounty of delights; and filling it gratified their desire to take part in the wild, exotic, romantic world outside.

The bedrooms of this era displayed massive oak beds patterned after Gothic cathedrals and spread with damask copied from Syrian fabrics of old. Front parlors specialized in carved sets of tufted horsehair furniture, walls papered with flocking, floors covered with blossom- scattered carpets, and all around a lavishness of eye-

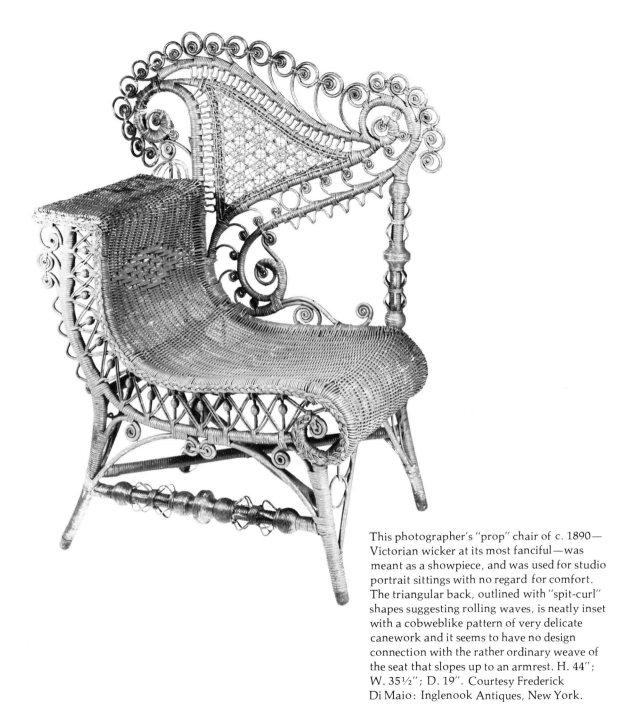

This photographer's "prop" chair of c. 1890—
Victorian wicker at its most fanciful—was
meant as a showpiece, and was used for studio
portrait sittings with no regard for comfort.
The triangular back, outlined with "spit-curl"
shapes suggesting rolling waves, is neatly inset
with a cobweblike pattern of very delicate
canework and it seems to have no design
connection with the rather ordinary weave of
the seat that slopes up to an armrest. H. 44";
W. 35½"; D. 19". Courtesy Frederick
Di Maio: Inglenook Antiques, New York.

Here, a little boy, all dressed up like a foreign officer, stands in front of a photographer's chair exactly duplicating the one seen in the previous illustration.
Courtesy Frederick Di Maio: Inglenook Antiques, New York.

Clarence John Laughlin's photograph, "Dream of Victoriana," 1963, is a valentine of the era, a romantic, mysterious, magical room with wicker "fancy" chairs, useful little tables, and an elaborately scrolled picture frame. The pieces are part of a collection of Victoriana that a Chicago woman, Mrs. Miriam Andreas, started early in the 1940s. She arranged this bedroom in her farmhouse in Illinois with a very special feeling for the period. The painting, propped against the pillows, of a woman in her nightgown has been called a "masterpiece of Victorian erotica": as the lady raises the gown with one hand, she hides her eyes with the other.
Photograph © 1973 by Clarence John Laughlin.

20

catching objects: porcelain figurines, portraits in gilt-edged frames, fringed runners of striped silk, decoupage boxes, cut crystal bottles, perhaps a stuffed owl, and lots that was lacy, fancy, and fantastic. There were ingenious pieces: before the advent of the bathroom there was something resembling an elaborately upholstered sofa that lifted up to reveal a full-length metal bathtub. And there were flamboyant touches: wicker chairs tucked into Turkish "cozy corners" dripping with tassels and rich hangings.

Wicker furniture was not kept to the corners only. Throughout the Victorian age wicker was popular, first for the porch and garden, then for the parlor, the bedroom , and the nursery; in the last quarter of the nineteenth century it was the absolute rage.

Wicker was homey, and that appealed to the Victorians. It was handmade and comfortable, unlike most furniture made after 1850, which was mass-produced and, on the whole, torturously uncomfortable. And wicker was exotic: it was Oriental in extraction, with a flexibility that allowed it to take on elaborate forms. The rattan, reed, and willow, of which most Victorian wicker was made, could be fashioned into the arabesques and curlicues that were the favorites, or styled in the Gothic, Rococo, or Chinese mode, to accent or meld with the parlor decor of eclectic furniture.

Before 1850, much of the wicker furniture available in America was imported from England and the Orient. By 1860, most of it was made here, although there was still a good market for special import pieces such as the peacock chair, first distributed by A. A. Vantine's of New York.

The rocking chair was not only an American invention (attributed by some to Benjamin Franklin), but it was also an American institution. Supposedly therapeutic, doctors sometimes referred to them as "digestive chairs." They were also recommended as useful to invalids. In the middle 1800s, an English writer reported in a travel book, "the disagreeable practice of rocking in the chair . . . how this lazy and ungraceful indulgence ever became general, I cannot imagine; but the [American] nation seems so wedded to it, that I see little chance of its being forsaken" (*The Encyclopedia of Victoriana*, ed. Harriet Bridgeman and Elizabeth Drury, London: Hamblyn, 1975).

With an eye to the fashionable decor of the time, this high-styled rocking chair expressed the "gothic" trend. Rather strict and controlled, with a square back and a minimum of curves, the design is both handsome and subdued. The cane seat, open patterned and handwoven, and the loop work around the arms and back indicate that the chair was made before 1880. H. 39"; W. 25¾"; D. 31½". Courtesy Frederick Di Maio: Inglenook Antiques, New York.

From the home of Mr. and Mrs. George Finch, St. Paul, Minnesota, 1881,
a very sentimental bedroom overflowing with knickknacks and personal
mementos. Wicker chairs are decorated with pretty bows and sashes;
pictures are festooned with fans and feathers; even the tea table is swathed
with gathered silk, bowed in satin, then draped with a fall of lace: a
Victorian's delight of creativity. Courtesy Minnesota Historical
Society, St. Paul.

Gervase Wheeler, in his lively little book, *Rural Homes* (1851), cites the company of Messrs. J. & C. Berrian of New York as being the major American manufacturer of wicker furniture at that time. Wheeler wrote: "A material now in very general use in this country, the rattan or cane of the East Indies, affords an immense variety of articles of furniture, so strong, light, and inexpensive, that it seems peculiarly adapted to general introduction in rural homes." In his stylebook he sketched thirteen illustrations of wickerwork made by the Berrians, and ventured that "the useful, the simple, and the elegant in form are the most beautiful attributes of every accessory of inner furnishing." The furniture shown had Gothic, French Rococo, and Chinese influences.

But it was not the Berrians who were to be remembered as the dominant force in the American wicker industry. It was Cyrus Wakefield and the Wakefield Rattan Company. Cyrus Wakefield began his working life as a grocer in Boston. The beginning of his interest in rattan has been recorded thus:

> One morning in the year 1844 a young man stood on a wharf in Boston watching the unloading of a vessel just arrived in port. A stevedore threw a small bundle of rattan over the railing of the ship. The moment for which the youth was waiting had evidently arrived and he hastened up to the mate and asked what he intended to do with the discarded rattan. He was told that it was of little value and served chiefly as ballast to prevent the cargo from shifting on its long voyage from the East. So he secured the rattan for a small sum, and, shouldering the burden, carried it to the grocery store on the waterfront which he and his brother conducted. The purchaser was Cyrus Wakefield, founder of the rattan and reed industry in this country, and this transaction was the beginning of a business which later became that of the Wakefield Rattan Company.

The account is from *A Completed Century, The Story of the Heywood-Wakefield Company, 1826-1926*, published by that company in their centennial year. There are conflicting versions of what Wakefield did with his first rattan. One story is that he wrapped an old rocker with it. Another story is that he sold it to basketmakers who

The "Turkish corner" was a craze in the 1890s. This contemporary version has curtained walls, quilted banquettes, and an oversized pouf made of sheets printed in a paisley design. The look is cozy and eclectic, a blending of modern and traditional things. The mantel and tabletops are filled with personal touches, and the vintage wicker chairs, circa late 1800s, seem to be an integral part of the romantic scene. The sheet pattern is Pastiche by Martex, from the 1977 Spring collection.
Courtesy West Point-Pepperell, Inc.

A girl's attic bedroom, all red and pink and orange and wicker—a simple
decorating solution that allows for a growing child's changing tastes
and interests. With different colors, cushions, curtains, or wallcoverings
the room will look entirely different, but the wicker will always remain the
same: pretty and functional. These pieces are thought to have been made
by Heywood Brothers and Wakefield Company in the late 1800s.
Interior design by Hilda Tarlow; photograph: Ernst Beadle.

Nineteenth-century wicker chairs lend their special country charms to a bedroom in a modern Manhattan apartment. They are graceful without being gaudy and seem to exemplify what Edith Wharton once wrote in 1897: "If little can be spent in buying furniture, willow armchairs will be more satisfactory than the 'parlor suit' turned out in thousands by the manufacturers of cheap furniture." *Photograph: Jennifer Sims.*

A little vignette of diverse pieces shows the wonderful range of shapes into which wicker was woven. The neat settee looks compact and restrained, while the red-lacquered side chair has a mildly sensuous air compared to the country hominess of the platform rocker. The rocking chair was an institution all across America by the first quarter of the nineteenth century. After visiting this country in 1838, James Frewin, an English builder, wrote, "It is considered a compliment to give the stranger the rocking chair as a seat, and when there is more than one in the house, the stranger is always presented with the best." *Courtesy Gloria Vanderbilt; photograph: Ernst Beadle.*

In the family sitting room white-lacquered wicker combines with gay chintz and simple gingham—a natural affinity. The harp design woven into the back of the rather voluptuous armchair seems to lighten the basketweave work that forms the bulky frame. During the late 1880s different motifs were used to add excitement to styles; the favorites were palms, fans and feathers, hearts, stars and sunbursts. In an age when there was no limit to innovation, the wicker industry gave full reign to new and imaginative ideas each year. *Courtesy Gloria Vanderbilt; photograph: Ernst Beadle.*

(ABOVE LEFT) Victorians loved plumpness and roundness. This armchair is a perfect example of the "full-bodied" look they favored, with its curvaceous lines and deep rolls of scrollwork ending in ornamental curls. It would seem to be just the sort of wicker that Ella Rodman Church recommended in *How to Furnish a Home* (1881): "a chair in which one can lounge in wrapper and unbound hair before the fire, and think over the events of the day that is past, or build air castles for the one to come." The spindly armchair facing it was probably known as a "lady's" chair—definitely feminine and fragile-looking—an occasional piece that was perhaps gilded in its earlier days and trimmed with satin bows and ribbons. *Courtesy Gloria Vanderbilt; photograph: Ernst Beadle.*

(ABOVE RIGHT) Tucked under a spiral staircase is a "cozy corner," much admired by the Victorians as an intimate and sociable place for tête-à-têtes. The stylized side chair in the foreground is decorated with a rich display of fancywork twines, spools, and curlicues—a valentine of pure whimsy and romantic design. The armchair is worked with swags of weaving at the legs to simulate draped fabric (probably to suggest demureness). *Courtesy Gloria Vanderbilt; photograph: Ernst Beadle.*

Violets in bloom and frosty white wicker turn this dressing room/bath into a garden of fresh delights. The handsome armchair in the foreground is the larger piece in scale and height, and in its day could have been meant for a gentleman's library. *Courtesy Gloria Vanderbilt; photograph: Ernst Beadle.*

The wickerwork in this armchair is a fine blend of delicate handweaving and timeless elegance. The flowing curves of the design look as sophisticated as sculpture, but beneath all the filigree work there is basic strength and sturdy comfort. As long ago as 1851 Gervase Wheeler, in his stylebook *Rural Homes*, admired wicker furniture for its "durability, elasticity, and great facility of being turned and twisted into an almost endless variety of shapes." *Courtesy Gloria Vanderbilt; photograph: Ernst Beadle.*

A penthouse terrace in Manhattan is treated like a country porch with a collection of old-fashioned wicker in Bar Harbor (square-back), Newport (heart-shaped back), and Southampton (curved-back) styles. The straw canopy, trailing wisteria, and simple plank flooring add to the turn-of-the-century ambience.
Interior design by Sandra Merriman; photograph courtesy The New York Times.

(OVERLEAF) This glassed-in terrace in Westchester County, New York, exemplifies the indoor-outdoor look for a country sitting room. The wicker furniture by Bielecky is a larger-scaled version of their Bar Harbor style, which was designed in the early 1900s.
Interior design and photograph by Angelo Donghia.

Angelo Donghia's guest room in Key West, Florida, sparkles with clear colors and natural textures. Furnishings are minimal; the look is airy, carefree, and casual. Buri armchairs, a bamboo table, roll-up shades, and straw matting seem to cool while keeping an appropriately tropical feeling. Sun hats, the hammock, a carryall, the fan, and the embroidered stole arranged along the wall are as decorative as they are functional. The object here and throughout the Victorian house was to create simple and refreshing spaces. *Interior design and photograph by Angelo Donghia.*

Sedate wicker rocking chairs cluster around an old-fashioned center table, a Mexican-inspired version of a look that was popular in Victorian parlors. Instead of lace over embroidered silk, the table is covered with a handwoven cloth. Instead of the family Bible, photograph albums, and fancywork bibelots, there is a huge vase of garden-fresh flowers. The delicate brass-and-glass hanging lamp and the embossed metal mirror add to the room's eclectic feeling. *Interior design by Easton-LaRocca.*

The peacock fan-back chair, first brought from China to America by clipper ships in the eighteenth century, is a favorite shape used everywhere today—in private houses as well as commercial establishments. It is a classic, available in various levels of workmanship at a wide range of prices, and every bit as popular as the Brighton chair, Thonet's rocker, and Mies van der Rohe's Barcelona chair. Over twenty-five years ago, when the Fong family came to California from Hong Kong, they began to manufacture this chair, called "Empress," and it is still in their catalogue, a continuous best-seller. H. 60″; W. 46″; D. 26″. *Courtesy Tropi-Cal, Los Angeles.*

Yards of white canvas and mats of straw bring summer-sunshine brightness to one-room living. Batik, bamboo, and rattan add Oriental flavor: crisp red-and-white cotton batik upholsters a bed that doubles as a sofa; modern Brighton chairs are scorched bamboo; the peacock chair is made of core and peel rattan. The paper-moon light, Japanese fan wallpaper in the window niches, and real bamboo growing in tubs also contribute to the Oriental spirit. *Interior design by Dean Drobyski; photograph: Ernst Beadle.*

Parsons-style canopy bed by Danny Ho Fong. Hardwood frame woven with peel rattan. The bed is an adaptation of the Billy Baldwin wrapped-willow styles developed in the 1950s. H. 84″; W. 45″; D. 81″; H. of side rail: 14″. *Courtesy Tropi-Cal, Los Angeles.*

The Tulip chair by Danny Ho Fong has great flair and style. Frame of 1¼″-diameter split rattan. H. 26″; W. 39″; D. 32″. *Courtesy Tropi-Cal, Los Angeles.*

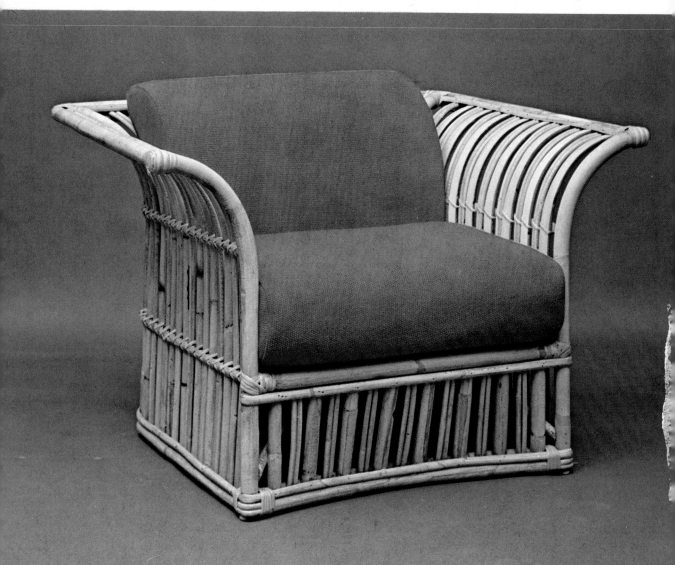

The elegant but substantial "mini-Empress" chair is built on an hourglass base in peel and then cross-woven of ⅜"-diameter rattan. For added strength, because the chair was developed for heavy-duty use in restaurants, there is a separate piece to support the back: rattan of a large diameter rolls around the structure from the base of the seat to frame the arms. Danny Ho Fong for Tropi-Cal. H. 27"; W. 24"; D. 23". *Courtesy Tropi-Cal, Los Angeles.*

This molded chair is of core rattan woven around a metal frame. Its futuristic shape, clean and functional, won an American Society of Interior Decorators award in 1965. Designed by Danny Ho and Miller Yee Fong for Tropi-Cal. H. 29½'; W. 33½'; D. 26". *Courtesy Tropi-Cal, Los Angeles.*

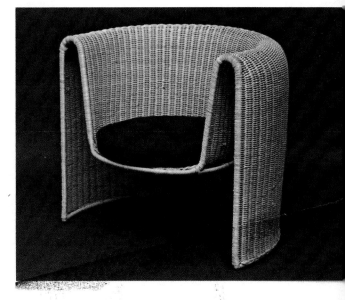

Thirty-year-old designer Waldo Fernandez custom-makes wicker furniture and heads his own decorating firm in Los Angeles. He advocates designing around natural materials; and although his own apartment was small and ordinary, he turned it into a visually exciting place by keeping to this premise. The eight-foot ceilings were heightened with vertical bamboo poles; giant baskets and plants also helped to give the illusion of a larger space. There are no lamps (the lighting hides behind plants and banquettes) or small tables to break up any open areas. *Interior design by Waldo Fernandez; photograph: Michael Olsen.*

In Waldo Fernandez's bedroom bold, six-inch-thick bamboo poles frame the beds, heighten the room, and are the strong, decorative elements in a clean expanse of space. Everything is kept simple: beds are covered in down-filled spreads made of inexpensive drapery lining; the night table and side chair are made of hickory; the floor is matted with sisal. And instead of graphics or pictures, a big, round basket tray is tacked to the wall. *Interior design by Waldo Fernandez; photograph: Michael Olsen.*

Here in Peter Rocchia's San Francisco home you can see in his wicker furniture the flow of design through history. His rounded, high-back chair is similar in form to the Roman basket chair of centuries ago. The closely woven furniture with the braided trim is reminiscent of the Madeiran wicker hearse sedan shown in the first chapter of this book. And yet his work is very much his own, and very much a wicker look for today.

Furniture by Peter Rocchia for The Wicker Works; photograph: Stone and Steccati.

Californian William Gaylord, known for his brilliant contemporary settings, used his up-to-the-minute knowledge of supertechnology to transform his own apartment, atop an 1890 Victorian town house. Gaylord's entire apartment space was gutted, then restructured with sleek, luxurious materials. His smooth, assured engineering is contrasted vividly with patterns and textures. Here, in his dining room, the 1930 Mies van der Rohe MR chairs add warm texture and sensuous shape to a rather austere surrounding. The table is two inches of marble supported by steel plates hidden in the chrome base. *Photograph: Russell MacMasters.*

Michael Taylor translates rather rustic elements—the cypress tree trunk, starfish and seashell, basket, "twig" art—into a sophisticated statement in the entrance of this California home. The "twig" art is by Arnoldi. The fretwork wicker chair is wrapped cane. *Interior design by Michael Taylor; photograph: Russell MacMasters.*

Michael Taylor created a clean and simple living space in this condominium overlooking the Pacific Ocean. By using lots of white and honeyed tones and one kind of furniture, he widened the room visually. Cushions are covered in white cotton; tabletops are pale travertine marble; floors are redwood that's been bleached and then lacquered for a high shine. *Interior design by Michael Taylor; furniture by Michael Taylor for Wicker Wicker Wicker; photograph: Russell MacMasters.*

Living with nature in a great big way is designer Michael Taylor's style of decorating. He brings the outdoors inside with his large-scale wicker furniture, green, growing plants, the fabulous stone floor. It is a totally American look, created with elemental materials. The Jennifer chair, designed especially for film actress Jennifer Jones, and plumped with oversized down pillows, is the size of a small sofa. The wicker table is shaped like a draped cover. *Interior design by Michael Taylor; furniture by Michael Taylor for Wicker Wicker Wicker; photograph: Charles Husted.*

stripped the rattan of its cane to get at the reed or pith they used in their weaving. The cane was then sold to chairmakers, who used it to make cane seats.

Whichever is the truth, Wakefield did recognize the commercial potential of rattan. The demand for cane was rising rapidly as cane-seated chairs became as fashionable in America as they had been in Europe the century before. But he also

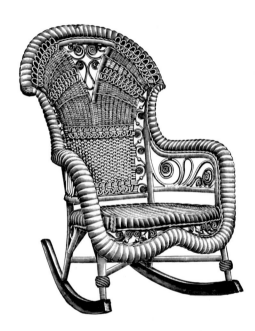

Ornate wicker satisfied the romantic and idealistic fancies of the 19th-century homemaker. The Heywood Brothers and Wakefield Company catalogues of the 1880s showed an incredible variety of styles and weaves, all handwoven and, of course, no two pieces were exactly alike. In 1879 the company sold over two million dollars worth of rattan furniture—an extremely high figure for the time, considering that an average chair cost only about three dollars. Courtesy Wakefield Historical Society, Wakefield, Massachusetts.

Massive tree trunks and green foliage provide a wraparound vista and a luxuriant background for an uncomplicated indoor environment of simple wicker furniture and granite-topped tables. The only sharp color is the red of the fat hand-screened fish pillow that sits on the sofa. *Interior design by Michael Taylor; furniture by Michael Taylor for Wicker Wicker Wicker; photograph: Russell MacMasters.*

realized that hand-stripping the rattan of its cane was an expensive proposition. He was fortunate to have a brother-in-law working in Canton, China, who helped him arrange the export of rattan and cane to Boston. This established Wakefield in quite a lucrative business.

The first rattan factory of the Wakefield Rattan Company was built in South Reading (now Wakefield), Massachusetts, in 1855; and that was where Wakefield's first wicker furniture was manfactured. In 1856 there was rebellion in China, a consequence of the Opium War, and rattan became unavailable for some time. Wakefield still had rattan in inventory, and he set to experimenting with the so-called waste materials—rattan shavings and reed.

With William Houston, a weaver from Paisley, Scotland, he devised and patented a process for spinning rattan shavings into yarn. Houston spun the first yarn for rattan matting in 1862, and the results went into floor coverings, window shades, and table mats. This phase of weaving became so successful that by 1881 fifteen varieties of brush mats were manufactured by the company.

Wakefield had known that reed could be used in the manufacture of baskets, but in working with it further, he found that it was also suitable for hoop frames (the cages that ladies wore under their skirts) and for wicker furniture. Wicker furniture made of reed had one spectacular advantage over rattan—it could be painted or stained, whereas shiny surfaced rattan resisted any finish but lacquer. It was this particular property, the fact that reed, plus being extremely flexible, could be curled and curved into extreme Victorian designs, that assured wicker's future popularity.

In 1875, the Wakefield Rattan Company bought out the smaller American Rattan Company in Fitchburg, Massachusetts; and twenty-two years later the company merged with the Heywood Brothers, whose business had started in 1826. Since 1870 Heywood Brothers had been the largest chair manufacturer in the country, famous for Windsor and bentwood chairs. But even with the merging of companies and the updating of machinery (to supply cane webbing for railroad and trolley car seats), the Wakefield Rattan Company had continued to make handwoven wicker furniture of almost unlimited design. When combined into one operation, the Heywood Brothers and Wakefield Company rapidly became the world's largest manufacturer of wooden chairs and school desks, wicker furniture, wicker baby carriages, baskets, and woven matting.

The chair pictured is a platform rocker, 1880-1890.
The base of the chair remains stationary, while the chair rocks
on supple steel rods attached to the axle. H. 47''; W. 28'';
D. 27½''. Courtesy Frederick Di Maio:
Inglenook Antiques, New York.

The Heywood Brothers and Wakefield Company shipped their orders by open truck in the 1880s. Courtesy Wakefield Historical Society, Wakefield, Massachusetts.

How it was at the Wakefield wickerworks before World War I according to *A Completed Century, The Story of the Heywood-Wakefield Company*, 1826-1926, published for the company.

In a large brick building bundles of rattan are received from the storage sheds. Here the rattan is weighed and submerged in troughs of cold water for about twenty minutes, as the soaking makes the fiber more pliable and easier to work. It is then picked up by an overhead conveyor and carried to an adjoining room where men sort it for quality and place it so that all the joints are in the same direction. This insures the scraping off of the rough joints when the outside of the rattan is split away from the core.

The parlor of a summer cottage in Oak Bluffs, Massachusetts, c. 1875, features a suite of dark-painted rattan furniture. The design of the wickerwork is highly unusual—somewhat reminiscent of French bistro chairs. Courtesy Smithsonian Institution, Washington, D.C.

Large bundles of graded rattan are carried on an overhead trolley to the splitting room, where there are groups of splitting machines in long parallel lines, with large piles of raw rattan beside each machine and racks in front piled with reed, and hooks hanging with bundles of cane.

The reed is the inside core of rattan and the cane is the outside hard skin. Each splitting machine is fitted with an ingeniously-designed set of knives. One blade scrapes the joints and another splits the skin of the rattan into a number of fine strands of cane, at the same time peeling them from the reed core. The cane and reed are tied in separate bundles and labeled according to grade, size, and variety. The reed is later dried overnight, weighed, and stored in sheds. The cane is transferred to an elevator and sent to the stockroom or directly to the shaving machines.

The shaving machines have four knives, two of which cut for thickness and two for width, and from these machines the rough and uneven strands of cane emerge in standard sizes. (The cane must be shaved accurately enough to gauge within one thousandth of an inch.) Simultaneously with the shaving, the number of feet produced is automatically registered.

The shaved cane is inspected, counted, and sorted according to length by "cane pullers." The bundles then go to the bleach house, where the cane is thrown over poles in brick vaults into which during the night sulphur fumes are forced from fire pots at each end. In the morning the cane is put outside to dry in the natural air.

The reed workers have stalls, their own private domains. Long reeds hang from the walls and there are stacks of frames ready to be woven. A supply of reed ready for work is kept in a bucket of water to make it pliable and to prevent splintering. The ends of the reed are pointed with a small knife so that they may be concealed when the piece is finished . . .

Fibre webbing (fibrecord of twisted paper) is stretched on the same kind of wooden frames that are used for reed furniture, and tacked by operators with hammer and nails, then finished off with braid.

In 1876, at the Philadelphia Centennial Exposition, the Wakefield Rattan Company received an award for their wickerwork: "for original design and superior workmanship in furniture, chairs, and baskets of an otherwise waste material; also for a new form of car seats, durable, cool, clean, and economical."

The Centennial Exposition was the great show that influenced the American homemaker and her ideas about decorating. Fifty-one countries displayed the products

The "drunken lord's chair" (c. 1810), an ingenious bamboo and cane chair with a built-in headrest and roll-out footstool, was made and exported by the Chinese, primarily to hot climates. It was much favored by Southern gentlemen, who, even in tropical heat, dressed in traditional wool breeches, flannel weskets, tweed jackets, and high leather boots. After a hard day's riding, they reposed and aired themselves on such a chair. In China the same chair was primarily used for lounging while smoking opium. H. 25"; L. 63" open. 40½" closed. Courtesy Museum of the American China Trade, Milton, Massachusetts.

of their arts and crafts, but the Orientals were the favorites by far. Never before had so many Americans—a reported ten million—seen such a profusion of Far Eastern wares and wonders. Most of all, they loved the bamboo. The Japanese ceramics on view were all set within ornamental enclosures of bamboo, and the exhibits of bamboo objects and furniture ranged from fans and screens, boxes and baskets, to stools and tables, chairs and settees.

In very little time the Oriental style became the rage in decorating. Lacquered boxes, carved ivories, miniature pagodas, countless fans, and silk embroideries were added to the happy confusion of bric-a-brac already installed on Victorian whatnots and mantelpieces. Fragile-looking, graceful bamboo furniture and wicker in the Chinese style, painted, gilded, or left natural, moved to the forefront in home decorating.

Bamboo had been an important look in decorating at the turn of the century before Victoria. In 1786, the Prince of Wales, "Prinny" as he was called, the future King George IV, uncle of the future Queen Victoria, bought a simple farmhouse in Brighton, which he transformed over the next thirty years into an Oriental extravaganza: The Royal Pavilion. It was a showcase for all the ravishingly beautiful chinoiserie he was fond of.

The great Corridor of the palace had an exuberance of bamboo. There were bamboo and cane fretwork armchairs, made in China, and slender consoles of beech simulating bamboo, made in England. The staircase was cast iron with a mahogany handrail made to look like bamboo.

In the corners of the Long Gallery, bamboo pedestals held porcelain figures, ceilings were lit with Chinese lanterns outlined with bamboo, and twelve different bamboo-patterned wallpapers covered the various walls. (These were designed for the Pavilion by the decorators, the firm of Crace and Sons.) The splendid bamboo furnishings went on throughout the palace, even to the future king's own bedroom where the simulated bamboo mixed in with the real, which included woven bamboo

An early 19th-century English colonial wardrobe with astonishing wickerwork ornamentation decorates the Paris bedroom of Léonor Fini, a creator of poetic settings for the ballet and theatre. Courtesy L'Oeil, Paris.

The Corridor or Long Gallery of the Royal
Pavilion, Brighton, was a magnificent
statement in chinoiserie, the finest example of
Chinese taste and furniture ever created in
Europe. The furniture was imported from
China through the Prince of Wales's
decorators, the firm of Crace and Sons. There
were "Japan Lacquer" cabinets, "very
handsome Sophas," chairs (including the tub
chairs we know today as Brighton chairs),
stools, and tables of bamboo, as well as great
quantities of porcelain. All the bamboo
furniture in the pavilion was made by the
Chinese expressly for export to the European
market. Friezes on tables and cabinets were
often ornamented with delicate canework,
which served the same purpose as ormolu
in European pieces. Courtesy The
Royal Pavilion, Art Gallery and
Museums, Brighton.

(LEFT) One of a pair of pedestals made in England c. 1818-1820 and placed in the Long Gallery of the Royal Pavilion on either side of the fireplace. The pedestal is in beech, bamboo, and porcelain with fret, rattan panels, a fish-scale pagoda roof, and brass gallery enclosing panels of Spode porcelain decorated with flowers in the Chinese style. Courtesy The Royal Pavilion, Art Gallery and Museums, Brighton.

(RIGHT) This bamboo armchair, decorated with canework, was made in China for export to the European market c. 1800. Considerable quantities of this kind of furniture were bought by the Prince of Wales in 1802 for the Brighton Pavilion. Courtesy The Royal Pavilion, Art Gallery and Museums, Brighton.

wastebaskets. The tub chairs of fretwork bamboo in the royal bedroom were a pair matching thirty-four others made especially for the Pavilion and known today as "Brighton" chairs.

Later in the nineteenth century, bamboo and wicker were part of the "aesthetic" trend in decorating. They were favored by young moderns busy adding "studio" touches to their homes.

The studio decor was copied after the artists of the day, especially James Abbott McNeill Whistler, who had long collected Japanese porcelains and whose exotic ideas and Oriental tastes were widely bruited about. Articles about his and other artists' studios—William Merritt Chase, Lawrence Alma-Tadema, and Robert Blum, to name three—in magazines such as *Harper's* and *Cosmopolitan* popularized their ideas of furnishing.

The Victorians thought it romantic to make a corner vignette with a folding screen, a bamboo chaise beside a silk-draped table, a big jar of peacock feathers, and a bamboo easel supporting a watercolor painting, although the carefully arranged still-life composition seemed to some a wild impossibility to add to the already abundantly appointed Victorian parlor.

The Decorator and Furnisher, a monthly magazine, published the following in 1882, an excerpt from an article by Kate Kirk on the subject of the new, eclectic decorating. The exchange is between Mrs. Newcomer and her grandmother, Mrs. Ouldtimson:

"Is this what you call a modern tea-room?" asked the old lady, taking a general survey of the apartment.

"Yes, Grandmamma, this is our tea-room."

"Will you inform me why those strips of matting are hung on the wall, instead of being on the floor?"

"Oh, Grandmamma," exclaimed Mrs. Newcomer in a horrified tone, "they are bamboo panels."

Mrs. Ouldtimson remained thoughtfully silent for a moment, then said: "And this is what you call cultivating a taste for the beautiful . . . ???"

With high Victorian flourish an ornate rocking chair has been embellished with all manner of weaving techniques: the cameo-shaped back is worked in a delicate snowflakelike pattern, while the gridwork and scroll crest topping gives an Oriental feeling. There is also an interesting combination of materials used—rope wraps the arms; the tiny braid that swirls around them is Hong Kong "grass"—a raffialike fiber. c. 1890. Note that the elaborate apron front extends to the sides, a type of construction not found in most rocking chairs. The curved seat is a rare feature of this chair. H. 41½"; W. 25"; D. 34". Courtesy Frederick Di Maio: Inglenook Antiques, New York.

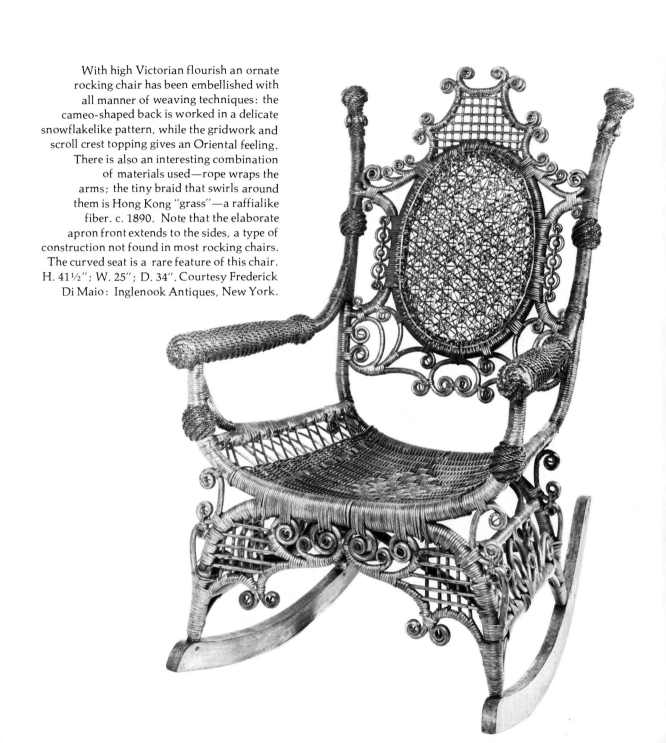

An 1895 entrance hall furnished like a sitting room almost expresses out loud the tapestry of a family's life. Looking at their possessions is like pouring through an old scrapbook: their grandfather's stuffed animal heads and rifles, grandmother's lace tea cloth and cut crystal ware, and a melange of comfortable wicker pieces scattered about. Colonial fire buckets hang from the heavy polished beams, and Oriental rugs (essential to proper Colonial interiors in the 1890s) add pattern to varnished floors. The sitting room glimpsed through a curtained doorframe is a continuation of mixed styles in decorating. With central heating, rooms began to flow together in a connecting series and to have mutliple uses, greatly increasing the livability of houses. Photograph of the entrance hall of Clonniel, the home of Dr. T. G. Morton of Strafford, Pennsylvania, courtesy Historical Society of Pennsylvania, Philadelphia.

Here, in the smoking room of J. A. St. John's home in Boston, you can glimpse the eclectic richness of the 1890s. The William Morris geometric wallpaper is the background for a lotus-print fabric, an Oriental rug, and wicker side chairs of the garden variety. More exotica is evident in the bamboo screen, a plaster monkey, and the picture of a lion posing in front of the fireplace opening. Even though the wicker is feminine looking, the owners have taken great care to make the room a man's domain. According to William Seale, an authority on Victorian times, gender became an important element in the decoration of rooms in the 1890s. Photograph by Charles Currier courtesy The Library of Congress.

"Art culture," said Mrs. Newcomer.

"I see an incongruous collection of modern and antique furniture," continued Mrs. Ouldtimson, "such as Turkish rugs and wicker chairs; a pine cupboard and an inlaid cabinet; and a superfluity of ornaments, one article destroying the effect of the other."

"I am sorry you do not admire our tea-room, Grandmamma, but we are only amateurs in esthetics . . ."

By the late 1880s eclectic decor was in full swing, with vast revivals in furniture available: Grecian, Elizabethan, Renaissance, Gothic, Moorish, Louis XVI. Virtually every historical style was represented and sometimes combined, even in the most gracious homes. The patterns and wonders of the Far East heightened the exotic and splendiferous look of interiors, and hominess was guaranteed with the addition of seashells and shawls, flowers of silk, and hand-painted fans.

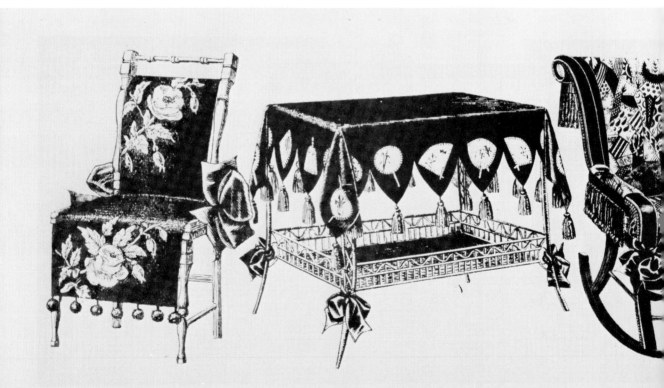

The Decorator and Furnisher was one of the arbiters of taste that sold for thirty-five cents a copy and offered drawings of interiors, colored plates of designs, articles on decorating, a column called "Hints and Notions," and advertisements (known as "puffs") that covered every commodity from oilcloths to steam pumps. In 1883 the magazine's editors reported "Heliotrope is to be the fashionable flower this season." "Spanish laces are no longer fashionable." "Private houses are now using electric lights. The residence of the Duke of Sutherland in England is fitted up with 250 lamps." "Chicken down is the name of the newest color, a delicate yellow." "Prairie dogs are to be utilized, their skins being highly recommended for upholstery uses." Articles from issues of 1882 and 1883 about the latest in furnishings made mention of wicker:

> Wicker chairs, which have become such favorites, are now painted in all colors, and when furnished with cushions are exceedingly pleasant to handle and to use. Some of the smoking chairs have pockets or baskets attached, a great convenience to a lazy reader.

"Fancy work" was the Victorian lady's obsession with decoration. Even wicker, already a feast of intricate design, was gilded or bronzed and further embellished with butterfly bows, silk tassels, and clever needlework. The side chair at left is gilded, its caned seat and back are covered with a scarf of embroidered velvet, fringed with plush balls, and bowed in stain. The wicker table has been transformed with a dark red felt cover, appliquéd with Japanese fans, and fringed with gold tassels. The cozy rocking chair has been "slip covered" with a length of crazy quilting created from silks, satins, and velvets. Courtesy Charles Scribner's Sons, from Frances M. Lichten, *Decorative Art of Victoria's Era* (1950).

The rattan lounges for a morning room are all the rage. Accompanying footstools are decorated with bright ribbons. Wastebaskets in split bamboo are now decorated with large bunches of artificial flowers tied on with gay ribbons. Occasionally variety can be obtained by the use of vegetables instead of flowers—bunches of spring carrots, asparagus, etc. . . .

The ribbons and flowers were a special touch added by the Victorian housewife, an expression of her individuality. Her home was her life, and there she gave full vent to whatever artistic talents she had. She turned out an abundance of handwork, including "fancy work"—decorative needlecraft into which she wove porcupine quills, bird feathers, seashells, leaves, pine cones, beads, rice, even locks of loved ones' hair. She crimped shreds of old woolens into lamp mats, twined wreaths of reddened vines to lay across barren mantelpieces, and fashioned rustic frames from twigs to border favorite prints.

Handmade things, the Victorian lady felt, made her home more personal and more enticing. Wicker, handmade of natural materials, comfortable as well as fashionable, lent itself well to her decorating schemes. She used lots of wicker. She had lots to choose from.

The Wakefield Rattan Company's catalogue of 1885 showed seventy-one different designs of rockers alone. Prices ran from two to seventeen dollars, unfinished; but all the pieces (including children's cabinets, rocking and highchairs, as well as bassinets and swinging cribs) could be shellacked or stained, enameled, gold-leafed, or bronzed. The braided, scrolled, latticed, spooled, twisted, or plaited wickerwork came in patterns of stars, sunbursts, palms, feathers, fans, hearts, and sailors' knots. Besides rocking chairs and children's furnishings, the catalogue displayed "fancy" stands, divans, tea tables, library tables, bookstands, bric-a-brac stands, music holders, piano chairs, lounges, couches, footstools, ottomans, and even dog baskets.

Rare now, this elaborate pedestal table, its highly curved legs
sprouting curlicues and rolling scrolls, was a standard
production piece when first made, around the 1890s, by
Heywood Brothers. H. 29½"; Diam. 22". Courtesy Frederick
Di Maio: Inglenook Antiques, New York.

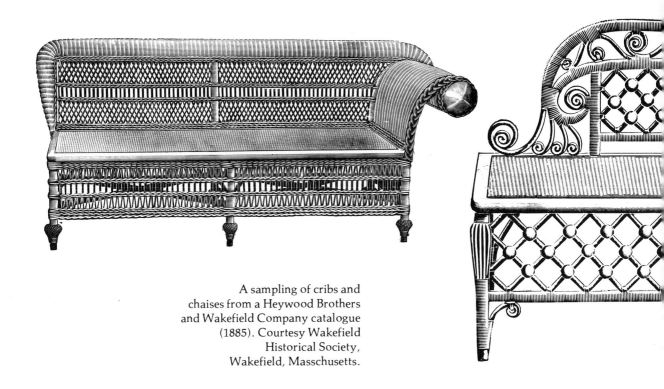

A sampling of cribs and
chaises from a Heywood Brothers
and Wakefield Company catalogue
(1885). Courtesy Wakefield
Historical Society,
Wakefield, Masschusetts.

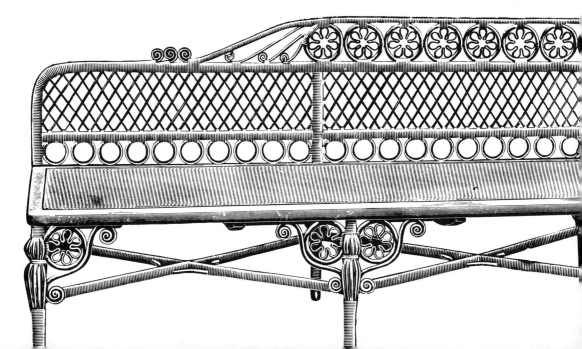

51

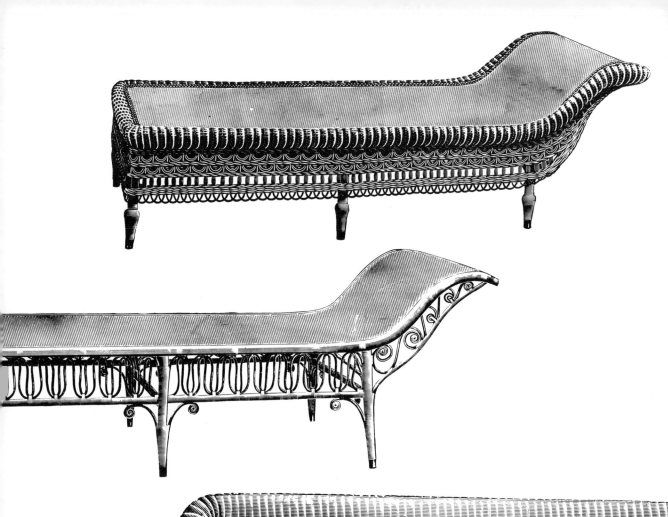

53

In 1895 Clarence Cook described an étagère in his book *The House Beautiful* as being "an ornamental upholder of the ornamental." In snug 19th-century interiors étagères or whatnots created yet another receptacle for stuffed birds, statuettes, wax flowers, and shell baskets so dear to Victorian ladies' decors. This particularly rare étagère is fashioned of natural wicker and is illustrated in the 1899 catalogue of Heywood Brothers and Wakefield Company. H. 63¼"; W. 24½"; D. 13¼". Courtesy Frederick Di Maio: Inglenook Antiques, New York.

The 1896 Sears, Roebuck & Company catalogue advertised fourteen wicker rockers. Number 9377 was described in this way:

> Our new $4.75 Ladies Reed Rocker. One of the swellest rockers out. Put this in your parlor and have the prettiest chair in your neighborhood. Give the four dollars we save for you on this rocker to your wife or put it in the bank. It's not often you can save that amount by a stroke of the pen. You will of course note that this rocker has full woven roll arms and a round back. The fancy pattern is of woven cane and rattan work, and is in imitation of a palm leaf fan. Full cane seat; fancy legs are wound and have handsome scroll work reinforcement. You know our terms. You see what the rocker is and that the price is away down. We expect your order.

If the lady preferred the rocker shellacked or stained, the price went up to five dollars and seventy cents.

But by 1895 ornate wicker was on the wane. There were too many designs. Oriental, Byzantine, Moorish, and Classical motifs had taken wicker furniture as far as it could go in exotica, leaving a legacy of styles called vulgar and grotesque by the advocates of good taste. There were too many colors and finishes—and too many ribbons. As Frances Lichten noted in *Decorative Art of Victoria's Era* (1950): ". . . when every piece of fashionable wicker was threaded with satin strands . . . there was nothing more that could be added, and the fashion for ornamentation died of its own absurdities."

Throughout the Victorian age there had been those who sought to temper the fads in decorating styles and to instill the superiority of simple tastes.

William Morris, the English architect, was a major reformer. He was designing furniture and fittings to suit his purist ideals in 1857; in 1861 he started his own decorating and designing business. His rule was: "Have nothing in your house that you do not know to be useful, or believe to be beautiful." The William Morris Company's first display at the International Exhibition of 1862 in South Kensington, England, showed delicate bamboolike furniture with rush seats, and hand-embroidered serge and linen textiles. Morris was a prodigious talent, and both the Art Nouveau and the German Bauhaus movements were indebted to his theories of art and decoration.

Another English architect, Charles Locke Eastlake, advocated hand craftsmanship and believed in common sense, comfort, and simplicity in decorating: "The best and most picturesque furniture of all ages has been simple in general form . . . sober in design, never running into extravagant contour or unnecessary curves." In 1872 he published his ideas in America in his book, *Hints on Household Taste in Furniture, Upholstery and Other Details.* The book instigated a widespread reform of furniture design, but it was not the reform he had hoped for. His well-intentioned edicts were unfortunately translated into some of the worst styles ever inflicted on the American market. Manufacturers invented a line of furniture "after Eastlake," which had nothing to do with the principles set forth in *Hints on Household Taste.*

This sewing basket of c. 1896 is the most elaborate of several models that were made by the Heywood Brothers and Wakefield Company. H. 31½"; W. 17½"; D. 14¼". Courtesy Frederick Di Maio: Inglenook Antiques, New York.

A play of textures: solid and tight weaving contrasts with the loose and airy in a side chair labeled Heywood Bros. & Co. (before the merger with the Wakefield Rattan Co. in 1896). The seat has machine caning framed with hardwood. The back is in a popular snowflake pattern. H. 39"; W. 18½"; D. 16½". Courtesy Frederick Di Maio: Inglenook Antiques, New York.

This rocking chair framed with closely woven rolled arms and back shows the individuality of its maker, who crafted a wrapped and scrolled sailboat for the chair back. Other motifs sometimes used in this way were banjos, harps, fans, and American flags. This chair was made around the 1890s and is a fairly rare example probably from Heywood Brothers. H. 37"; W. 27"; D. 30½". Courtesy Frederick Di Maio: Inglenook Antiques, New York.

Wicker and wood are combined in a novelty chair from the 1870s. The distinctive curved piece that outlines the back is one strip of rattan threaded with wooden balls. Bamboo frames the back, which contains a geometric inset of lacy intricacy woven with several sizes of cane. The legs of the chair are maple turned to simulate bamboo, while the stretchers are made of natural bamboo. The seat is made of closely woven pressed cane made by machine. H. 39½"; W. 22½"; D. 18". Courtesy Frederick Di Maio: Inglenook Antiques, New York.

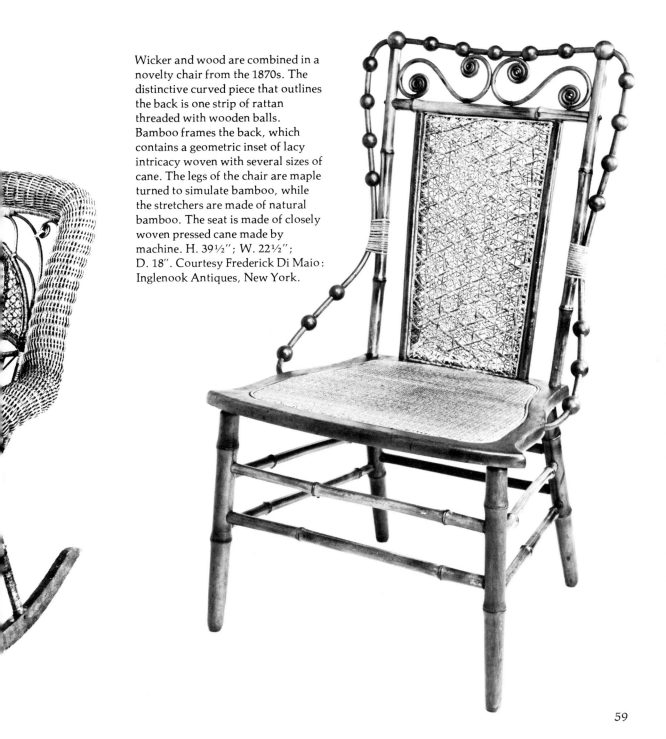

Cornelius Vanderbilt's veranda at the original Breakers before it burned to the ground in 1892. The wicker is embellished with macrame and silk tassels, swagged, upholstered, and cushioned for an opulent Oriental look. The canopied settee is draped in striped cretonne in the Turkish mode. The "sentry" chair with macrame sun shield is lined and upholstered in velvet. Courtesy Redwood Library and Athenaeum, Newport, Rhode Island.

In the old Casino Theatre at Broadway and 39th Street in New York City (1889) box stall patrons were seated in pretty white-painted wicker chairs of varying designs. Note the exuberant "Moorish" decoration. Photograph: Byron. Courtesy the Museum of the City of New York.

This homey Boston parlor, photographed in 1900, shows a wonderful assemblage of fabrics and furniture styles from a wide range of periods. The pale striped wallpaper and electrified chandelier were considered modern at that time. The wicker corner chair, lacquered dark brown and with a plush velvet seat cushion, was probably a prop for a Victorian photographer's studio. The overstuffed Turkish chair could be from the late 1880s; it has been reupholstered in yellow silk damask. The armless slipper chair was perhaps made in the 1870s and newly updated with bright chintz. The mahogany roundabout chair in the center of the room looks as if it was pulled from some other and more logical place just for the photograph. Oriental rugs, patterned silk cushions, Moorish tables, and a collection of pictures all come together quite agreeably. The effect is restrained and rather bare compared to the heavy-handed decoration seen in parlors of the late 1880s.

Yet there were true believers. Gustav Stickley was one of the most important. By 1900 Stickley was producing furniture of revolutionary design. He worked in oak and in willow, with which he wove his squarely compact wicker. His styles were the absolute antithesis of the curvaceous abandon that had prevailed just a few years before.

Victorian wicker was still around in the early 1900s, although you would be more likely to find it in some dusty retreat than showing off as the most prominent piece in the parlor. But even parlors were on the way out, a "living room" was the new idea. And Stickley's new look in wicker moved right in.

A rattan chair, French Second Empire, 1852-1870, from the collection of Jacques Rotil. Courtesy P. Devinoy; ©1973 P. Devinoy.

WICKER
IN THE TWENTIETH
CENTURY

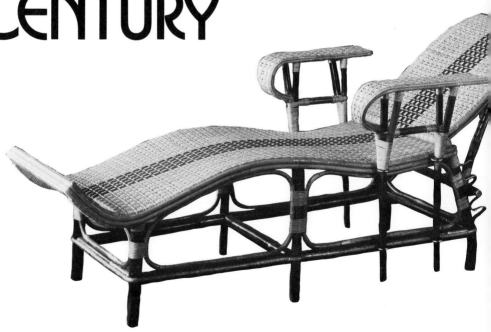

The new look in wicker was called Craftsman, which was Gustav Stickley's own name for the furniture he designed—or Mission, a style connotation started by mass merchandisers to describe sturdy, practical-looking furniture on the order of what might have been found in Franciscan missions in the American Southwest. Craftsman or Mission (the terms came to be synonymous) was truly a popular new look, not just for wicker, but for wood furniture as well.

As the nineteenth century approached the twentieth, the Victorian taste for the romantic and ornamental in home decorating was chastened by the modern appeal of functional furnishings, clean and pure of line. Wicker in the Craftsman or Mission design was sedate and studious. As before, it was still reasonable in price, handmade, well suited for indoors or out—and a decorative addition to any room, be it den, living room, playroom, bedroom. But it was no longer celebrated for the exotic forms it could take. It was celebrated for itself, in all its skillfully woven, simple beauty.

The early 1900s library of Charles H. Russell's home Oaklawn in Newport, Rhode Island, was decorated with what was then considered conservative and comfortable—a William Morris wallpaper, Oriental rug, bamboo chair and tables, along with a fancy striped-silk side chair and a down-to-earth, leather-upholstered wicker chair. Velvet side curtains separate the library from the parlor, through the arched doorway. The parlor is a more feminine room, with pastel wallpaper, French Louis XVI-type furniture, and flower-cushioned wicker. Courtesy Newport Historical Society, Newport, Rhode Island.

Frank Alvah Parsons, president of the New York School of Fine and Applied Art and an authority on interior decoration, felt that wicker was as important to a room as an antique piece of furniture. In his stylebook, *Interior Decoration: Its Principles and Practice* (1915), he described his idea of a modern living room "in which personality and charm result in a happy selection and combination of simple, unrelated objects in period and materials: an old pine cupboard bleached white, Heppelwhite side chairs, an early American cherry table—all mixed with simple wicker furniture." It's the eclectic sense of decorating again; but this time reflecting a clearly defined, highly individualized taste. Americans were becoming more sophisticated in aesthetics.

Good taste in decorating was an ongoing subject in books and magazines devoted to reforming the excesses of the late Victorians. William Morris and Charles Eastlake had been waging that battle for years. And in 1900, Gustav Stickley began his own crusade against what he called "Victorian imitation palaces filled with gilt complexes."

Stickley was a talented and ambitious man. He was born on a farm in Wisconsin in 1857, the eldest of eleven children. At seventeen he went to work in his uncle's chair factory in Brandt, Pennsylvania; by the time he was twenty-one he had become manager and foreman of the business. He went on to work in a number of furniture stores and factories, then in partnership, before he formed the Gustav Stickley Company in Eastwood, New York, in 1898. He took as his inspiration in design the simple, well-crafted styles of Shaker furniture; and he marketed his products, along with his design philosophy, through *The Craftsman*, which he began to publish in 1901. *The Craftsman* was a very original service magazine that undertook to guide average middle-income Americans in their search for moderately priced, good-quality furnishings and home designs. Although the earliest issues did not contain his designs for homes, the contents of the magazine soon included house plans and building materials; landscape and gardening ideas; news of paints, textiles, household appliances, lighting fixtures, and metalwork; along with how-to features and decorating articles. The whole magazine was dedicated to bringing the house and everything in it into harmony with its surrounding environment.

Stickley revered honest craftsmanship and straightforward design, and he made furniture that lived up to his ideals. He worked in native oak and willow almost exclusively, believing that they were the two most human and honest of materials—and particularly responsive to his basic rectangular shapes. His revolutionary work was first exhibited in 1900 at a trade show in Grand Rapids, Michigan, and it represented a direct about-face in furniture designing. Wooden pieces were handmade, constructed along strong, quiet lines; the finish was matte brown instead of the high gloss that had been common in American-made furniture; and the leather upholstery was smooth, with a soft glow, instead of being shiny and tufted. Willow pieces were crafted along the same angular lines, woven with straight, squared-off backs and arms, clean of line and pared down to what Stickley believed were the essential "bones" of the designs. Although wicker was of secondary importance to the more serious Craftsman styles in wood, it was just as important to Stickley's advocacy of total simplicity in home decorating.

Craftsman was the first popular modern furniture that the United States produced, and Stickley was the first American designer to build furniture on structural principles. The time was right for his plain and sensible furniture. It filled, in the most natural and direct way, the real needs of the American home: it was comfortable, durable, and easily taken care of. Stickley also believed it filled an emotional need: "the people were on the verge of an artistic awakening, a reaction against the insincerity and false ornateness of the furnishings of that [the late Victorian] period" (*The Craftsman*, catalogue, 1912). Ideas about home decoration were moving away from the fusty Victorian parlor toward the comfortably furnished, family-oriented living room. Craftsman or Mission wicker was appealing not only because it was sturdy and honest in line, but also because it was rustic and homey in feeling. Rustic meant country, and getting out into the country was what Americans began to do.

By 1905 the automobile was quite reliable, and streetcars traveled from city centers to open land where residential suburbs began to grow. Industry moved in downtown and the middle classes moved out into simpler settings, propelled by the desire to experience the new country culture. Sports—sailing, tennis, bicycling, and swimming—and outdoor life had become popular as well as fashionable; the first country clubs opened their doors. Clothing reflected the change, too: women's dresses were softer, less restricting. For men, frock coats were out, and top hats, long a symbol of the middle-class gentleman, were replaced by bowlers, boaters, and traveling caps.

People also went into the country to search for "makeovers"—finding stables,

From the 1912 Craftsman
Furniture Catalog. Courtesy Beth
and David Cathers.

71

From issues of *The Craftsman* for 1907 and 1913.

VERANDA DAYS

No. 1. For a screened porch which is the summer living room, a lamp is needed, and a wicker one is most appropriate, finished in the same color as the furniture or in contrasting hue.

No. 2. A settee is a desirable piece in that it takes up less space than two chairs. They are made to match any of the wicker styles on this page.

No. 3. Among indispensable small pieces is a pretty willow stool with a gay cushion.

Nos. 4-5. Of different styles but equally pleasing are these reed chairs. No. 5 is charming in light green with pale mauve rim and cushions of block printed linen to match.

Nos. 6-7. Firm in construction but light and graceful in effect, this table and rocker are of the same pleasing design. They are stunning when enameled in yellow with the border braid in black or in solid forest green.

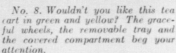

No. 8. Wouldn't you like this tea cart in green and yellow? The graceful wheels, the removable tray and the covered compartment beg your attention.

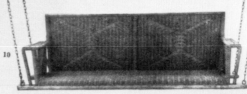

No. 9. To be a real haven of rest the porch must include a luxuriously comfortable chaise longue. This one is French willow in lustrous silver gray, the cushions of gray and mulberry with black.

No. 10. A swing hung across one end adds much to the comfort and appearance of a porch, especially when it is as attractive as the one here shown.

barns, chicken houses, and mills to renovate—and for the new sport of antiquing around the countryside. A whole industry of salvage yards, junk shops, and auction sales sprang up to supply goods for the new-old surroundings. "Quaintness" took the place of rusticity, and it was said that the "wealthier the people, the more they go in for the new fashion for quaintness." It wasn't smart to have bandbox-bright-looking things: fabrics were produced in pale, time-faded shades such as mulberry, old rose, gray-green, and pale watery gold. Antique satin was a best seller; antique white paint, an ivory or oyster shade, was the choice color for walls. Found (and newly bought) furniture was crackled to make it look as if it had weathered many a bleak winter and scorching summer; or it was painted (to look "cottagey") with two colors: subdued leaf green edged with putty gold or deep peacock banded with a striping of black. Wicker was two-toned, with stone green glazed over brighter green being the preferred antiquing colors. The effect was called a "delightfully cozy used look."

The kings of American industry moved into simpler settings as well. It was noted that

> aristocrats regularly left for a hill camp where they could revitalize their city bones with rusticity. Mission furniture, along with its attendant wicker, was of this porch and fireplace-oriented past-time. How else can we explain an Astor or a Rockefeller hiring Gustav Stickley to furnish their country homes in the Hudson Valley . . . (John Crosby Freeman, *The Forgotten Rebel*, Watkins Glen, N.Y.: Century House, 1966)

Stickley's popularity added to wicker's prestige as a material for furniture. *The Craftsman* printed numerous articles on the quiet styling, beauty, and versatility of wicker furniture. As Stickley increased his empire, his design credos were even more influential.

In May 1910 *Vogue* magazine published an article, "The Summer Home in America," giving decorating suggestions and noting that "Craftsman or Mission furniture makes a good effect in a simple bungalow or quaint cottage." The article went on to say that the addition of Stickley-type "comfortable and artistic" wicker furniture should complete the tasteful furnishings.

You didn't have to buy Stickley-made wicker to get simple, well-designed wicker furniture. The market was full of other good American-made pieces and imports of ex-

From the April 1918 issue of
Style in Home Furnishing.

cellent quality. *Vogue* frequently editorialized wicker furniture with pictures and articles after the turn of the century. In an August 1908 "Seen Around the Shops" column the magazine assured readers that they could find plenty of wicker pieces "which never need to be relegated to the attic because they are 'out-of-date.' " And by June 1912 *Vogue* said, "wicker, rattan, grass in natural tones or stained in out-of-door colors have usurped the place of wood for summer furnishings."

An early 1900s catalogue from Joseph P. McHugh's of New York (one of Heywood-Wakefield's big competitors) showed over one thousand sketches of Mission-styled wicker designs. The Grand Central Wicker Shop of New York, whose slogan was "In Reed We Lead—In Willow Others Follow," sold wicker all over North and South America to private customers and public country clubs, resorts, hotels, and theatres. It wasn't the Mission look, but it was plain and simple wicker. In those days the grand hotels and the fabulous resorts set trends in architecture and interior decora-

The Canton chair, as pictured in a 1913 advertisement for Vantine's, The Oriental Store. H. 37"; W. 18". Courtesy Cooper-Hewitt Museum, New York.

Julia Ward Howe, author of "The Battle Hymn of the Republic," was 91 years old in 1910, the year this picture was taken in Newport, Rhode Island. She was attending a suffragette rally at Marble House staged by the owner and the nation's leading suffragette, Mrs. Alva Smith Vanderbilt Belmont, who is standing behind the wicker invalid chair. The attendant gentleman is unidentified. Courtesy Brown Brothers, Sterling, Pennsylvania.

From the January/February 1904 edition of *The International Studio*, examples of modern Austrian wicker furniture designed by well-known Austrian artists, H. Funke and Hans Vollmer. In the late 1820s the Austrian government trained teachers in basket weaving and sent them to instruct villagers in the different Crown lands in that art, which later included the weaving of basket furniture. The program was initiated to provide villages with an income during the winters when there was no agricultural work. It continued through the 1900s, with teachers being first trained at the Imperial School in Vienna, under the Austrian Museum, and then sent to Bohemia, Austrian Poland, Croatia, Carinthia, and Moravia. These district schools produced large quantities of basket furniture for the foreign market. Their designs were copied from old patterns, patterns from the East, and new patterns by H. Funke, an artist and the director of the schools. The largest village engaged in this home industry was Rudnik, Poland, where thousands were employed, as in Prague. When there was an

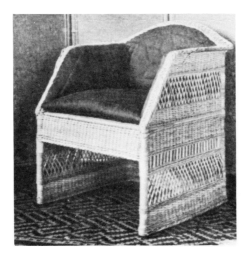

upheaval in art in Vienna in the late 1890s, the
first effort of the Prag-Rudniker firm was to
create a demand for something new in
basketwork furniture. Hans Vollmer, a pupil
of the artist Josef Hoffmann, was engaged
to devote himself to designing wicker
furniture. The products were shown at
the "Secession" exhibitions, as well as at the
Austrian Museum.

Six comfortable, unpretentious armchairs, designed in Germany, woven in willow, and lauded in a 1912 *Craftsman* article: these chairs "prove that good firm construction underlying a plain form of weaving has an unmistakable air of superiority far removed from the usual elaborate type of willow chair. The entire absence of ornamentation gives them a distinction, a dignity which no amount of intricate trimming could achieve."

From *Good Furniture,* June 1915. "A new type of American furniture in which willow is used in an entirely decorative sense, as panels set in a light ash framework." Furniture made by Joseph P. McHugh & Sons, New York.

tion. They used lots of wicker, and the wicker came to be called by the different resort spots with which it was associated: Cape Cod, Bar Harbor, Southampton, Newport.

Oriental-design wicker was still being imported from the Far East up until World War I. The Canton chair was the favorite sold by A. A. Vantine's in New York, the largest importer of wicker from the Orient. High-quality Austrian, German, and English wicker, as modern as any wooden-built furniture, also added to the influx of wicker designs from abroad. In 1904 *The International Studio* published a spread on Austrian wicker, remarking that the furniture was designed by well-known artists in high-styled novelty patterns with leather upholstery. (Later, in 1912, *The Craftsman* printed illustrations of German wicker furniture showing angular structural lines more simplified than the earlier Austrian or Stickley designs.) English imports of the early 1900s were developed at the Dryad Works in Leicester by Charles and Albert Crampton, descendants of a British basketmaking family. The designs were expansive and big-scaled, with flaring arms, rounded backs, and full-length skirting. Dryad cane furniture was imported exclusively by W. & J. Sloane in New York, who advertised it as made of the strongest unbleached pulp cane, without the use of nails or tacks.

Although Stickley wasn't the only designer of furniture in the new style, he was certainly the most influential one, at least in America. He was also one of the most influential figures in America's home-building industry. The ideal house, as Stickley envisioned it, was an all-American-made home, comfortable and efficient, and within reach of middle-class pocketbooks. His idealistic credo was to produce the highest quality of craftsmanship at the lowest prices for the most people. He preached bungalow living as a democratic, healthful way of life. In *The Craftsman* Stickley wrote that subscribers had asked him to design homes that were "simple, durable, and planned for genuine comfort" to go along with his furniture styles. He drew up plans for bungalow houses, the likes of which had never before been built in America, to fulfill the needs of readers. Stickley's typical one-story bungalows had casement or picture windows, big fireplaces, screened porches, children's playrooms, cheerful kitchens with built-in storage cabinets, and family-oriented living rooms.

Stickley built his first bungalow in 1908 on six-hundred acres of land he bought in Morris Plains, New Jersey. He furnished it throughout with Craftsman furniture, fixtures, and textiles. He designed his own extensive produce gardens, started a vegetable market and a dairy, and began a farm school for young boys, a kind of 4-H operation to teach them the principles of his beliefs.

About 1909 Craftsman furniture was at the height of popularity. *Masculine, virile,* and *boxlike* were words used to describe the Craftsman look, and indeed, there was nothing curvaceous about the styling. John Crosby Freeman, Stickley's biographer, wrote that the furniture "nearly growled with maleness." The wicker pieces, however sedate and solid-looking, had none of the heaviness associated with Craftsman oak. The settles and chairs, side tables and footstools were extremely contemporary,

Gustav Stickley, Architect.

without scrollwork or ornamentation, but when the pieces were mixed in with Crafts-man or Mission wood furniture, the effect was to lighten and soften interiors. A *Craftsman* article in 1912 explained that the wicker provided relief to the wooden fur-niture and prevented too serious an air.

In 1913 Stickley opened a unique twelve-story home-building center. He had

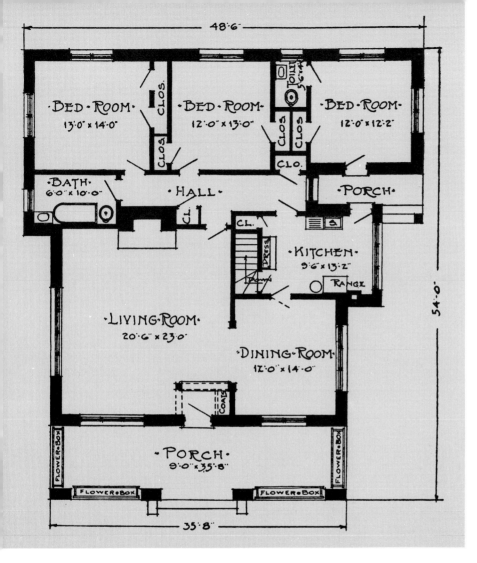

Floor Plan Labels

- ·BED·ROOM· 13'·0" x 14'·0"
- CLOS.
- ·BED·ROOM· 12'·0" x 13'·0"
- TOILET 5'·x 4'·4"
- CLOS
- CLOS
- ·BED·ROOM· 12'·0" x 12'·2"
- ·BATH· 6'·0" x 10'·0"
- CLO.
- ·HALL·
- CL.
- ·PORCH·
- CL.
- PRESS
- ·KITCHEN· 9'·6" x 13'·2"
- RANGE
- ·LIVING·ROOM· 20'·6" x 23'·0"
- ·DINING·ROOM· 12'·0" x 14'·0"
- COATS
- FLOWER BOX
- ·PORCH· 9'·0" x 35'·8"
- FLOWER BOX
- FLOWER·BOX
- FLOWER·BOX
- 48'·6"
- 54'·0"
- 35'·8"

A six-room Craftsman bungalow, designed by Gustav Stickley, with fieldstone, long porch, and compact homelike interior. Number 167, from the August 1913 issue of *The Craftsman* magazine. Courtesy Jordan-Volpe Gallery, New York.

opened The Craftsman Building at 41 West 34th Street, New York, in 1905, where he housed his executive and editorial offices. These were moved to the second building, at 6 East 39th Street, as soon as it was ready. The first two floors of the new Craftsman building were furniture showrooms; the next two displayed textiles, glass, pottery, tapestries, rugs, and art. The fifth floor had actual gardens planted with grass, shrubs,

Wicker in the Mission style decorates the breakfast porch of Mrs. Roger Straus, Purchase, New York. The advertisement appeared in the October 1915 issue of *Arts and Decoration.* Courtesy Cooper-Hewitt Museum, New York.

and flowers, and was decorated with fountains and pergolas. Floors six through eight were given over to the permanent Craftsman Home Builders Exposition, where more than eighty exhibits showed metalwork, fabrics, building materials and methods, paints and finishes, wall coverings, garden tools, and miniature house models. Above this *The Craftsman* offices were housed. To the public this was all impressive enough, but the most talked-about department was the restaurant on the top floor, where fresh food and sparkling spring water were rushed daily by trucks from Craftsman Farms.

For less than two years Stickley enjoyed the magnificence of The Craftsman Building and the power of his position in the industry. In March 1915 a petition of bankruptcy was filed against The Craftsman, Inc., and a receiver appointed. (The Craftsman, Inc., was an amalgamation of all the Stickley properties, including his stores, mills, and factories.) Mary Ganton Roberts, managing editor and art editor of *The Craftsman*, wrote in the last issue of the magazine that Stickley had "dreamed too fast for the world."

Stickley had also overextended himself in business, but his bankruptcy was certainly aided by the proliferation of inexpensive (and inferior) copies of his designs and

A *House & Garden* article in 1917 showed the quaint look "forty-five seconds from Broadway"—a cottage in a New York flat, the apartment of Louis Fancher, illustrator. Courtesy Cooper-Hewitt Museum, New York.

Around the turn of the century wicker began to be made in matching sets. It was a new idea, and it had lasting popularity. This is a porch—or "outdoor living room"—furnished with wicker sets from the Boston Willow Furniture Company in 1918. Courtesy Cooper-Hewitt Museum, New York.

by the revival of the early American Colonial style in furniture. He withdrew from the furniture industry and spent the rest of his life experimenting with wood finishes.

The Mission style still prevailed, though, for wicker furniture, along with all the other plainer weaves that wicker manufacturers had been specializing in since the turn of the century. But it was really only a few years more before finely crafted wicker was all but withdrawn from the furniture industry.

Back in the early 1900s, wicker manufacturers had started to develop open-weave designs. Labor was expensive, and the open work took much less time to complete than the very popular close weaves. In 1904 a machine was invented that spun twisted paper from wood pulp. The product was called fiber, a highly pliable material that was resistant to breakage. It needed no soaking for flexibility, and it was strong, having been

Machine-made wicker baby carriage shown in a 1920s Heywood-Wakefield catalogue. The company operated three factories that produced only baby carriages. Wicker was always the preferred material, because of its sanitary and ventilating properties. This fanciful takeoff on the Ford motorcar was complete, right down to the license plate. Courtesy Wakefield Historical Society, Wakefield, Massachusetts.

A 1919 Perféktone wicker phonograph cabinet from the Heywood Brothers and Wakefield Company. With the rising tide of prosperity in 1915, there came a demand for high-priced phonographs, and salesmanship centered on cabinetry and styling. Perféktone cabinets were advertised as "the last word in acoustical science as applied to sound-reproducing instruments, having no confined air spaces or cavities to destroy the original coloring of the music." The reed and cane cabinet was said to eliminate completely the countervibrations so noticeable with wood cabinets. Courtesy Wakefield Historical Society, Wakefield, Massachusetts.

This settee from Karpen Brothers, which appeared in an article in *Good Furniture* magazine in June 1925, is woven French cane, a novelty of design, weaving, and color combinations.

A classic-style reed chair by the Bielecky Brothers, 1925. From *Good Furniture*, June 1925.

treated with a glue sizing that stiffened it and helped it to retain its shape as furniture. It was also extremely inexpensive. Wicker manufacturers could use the very cheap fiber to produce closely woven wicker furniture, and the low price of the material would offset the high cost of labor. But most manufacturers in those days still preferred the naturals—reed or willow.

During and after World War I economic conditions brought about greatly increased import duties on reed. The Department of Agriculture attempted to create a domestic willow-raising industry, but was not successful. So with the raw material priced sky-high, and with the expensiveness of labor, natural, handcrafted wicker furniture couldn't compete with the newest idea to hit the market: machine-woven wicker from man-made fiber.

(LEFT) The hourglass chair and matching porch furniture, imported by A. A. Vantine's, 1925. From *Good Furniture*, June 1925.

(ABOVE) A favorite design of the 1920s, round reed with lozenge ornaments, by Ficks Reed Company, New York. From *Good Furniture*, June 1925.

(LEFT) An unusual "console" set— even the candlestick holders match. By Ficks Reed Company, New York. From *Good Furniture*, June 1925.

In 1917, Marshall B. Lloyd, a manufacturer of baby carriages, invented and perfected a machine that wove wicker furniture from the less expensive, more flexible fiber. The machine was called the Lloyd loom, and it could do the work of thirty men. There wasn't a wicker manufacturer who could touch his closely woven furniture in cost of manufacture or price to consumer. In 1921 the Lloyd Manufacturing Company of Menominee, Michigan, was made a wholly-owned subsidiary of the Heywood-Wakefield Company (formerly the Heywood Brothers and Wakefield Company), which bought the loom patent as well. By then, almost fifty percent of all wicker furniture produced in America was made of fiber, and by 1930 the figure had climbed to eighty-five percent.

There was only one area where real handmade wicker was firmly in demand— the

(RIGHT) The wicker pilot seat in Charles Lindbergh's plane, "Spirit of St. Louis." Courtesy National Air and Space Museum, Smithsonian Institution, Washington, D.C.

(FAR RIGHT) This advertisement appeared in *The Newport Bulletin*, July 1930. Courtesy Newport Historical Society, Newport, Rhode Island.

airplane industry. Interest in air travel boomed during the 1920s, and because wicker was the lightest material known (even lighter than twisted paper fiber), it was used exclusively for pilot and passenger seats in early airplanes.

Perhaps the uniformness of fiber, the repetitive styling, and the very fact that it was machine-made and looked it, helped bring wicker down from its fashionable heights. Also, there were other and newer American materials for "leisure" furniture: plastic, chrome, polished metal tubing, and wrought iron replaced wicker in the sunrooms and on terraces. Matched sets of chunky-shaped rattan looked more contemporary in the 1930s and could be found in dens and rumpus rooms, the second living room in suburban homes.

Natural, handwoven, highly individual wicker, in the Victorian style and in the

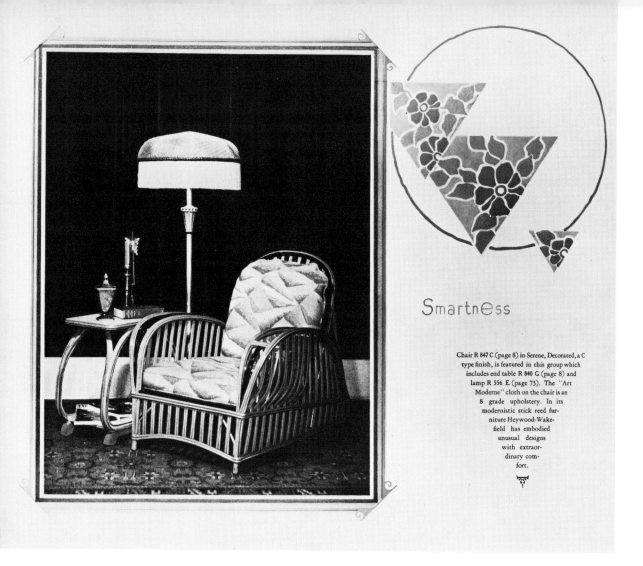

Smartness

Chair R 847 C (page 8) in Serene, Decorated, a C
type finish, is featured in this group which
includes end table R 840 G (page 8) and
lamp R 556 E (page 73). The "Art
Moderne" cloth on the chair is an
8 grade upholstery. In its
modernistic stick reed furniture Heywood-Wake-
field has embodied
unusual designs
with extraor-
dinary com-
fort.

From the Heywood-Wakefield catalogue of 1929. Photograph courtesy Frederick Di Maio:
Inglenook Antiques, New York.

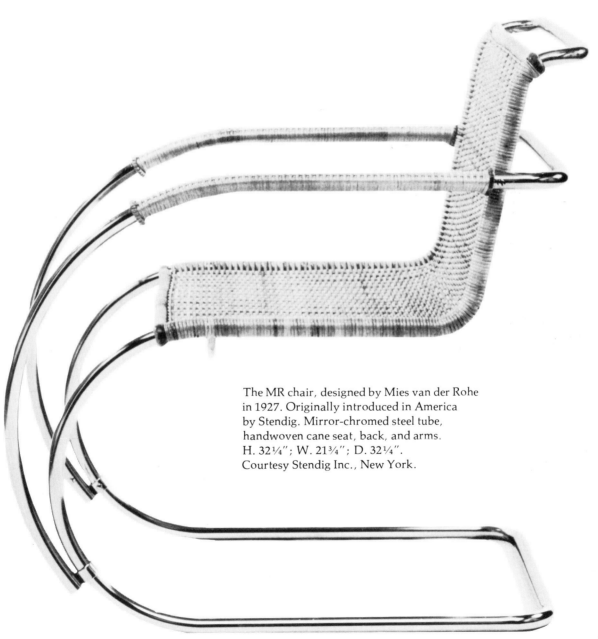

The MR chair, designed by Mies van der Rohe
in 1927. Originally introduced in America
by Stendig. Mirror-chromed steel tube,
handwoven cane seat, back, and arms.
H. 32¼"; W. 21¾"; D. 32¼".
Courtesy Stendig Inc., New York.

"modern" styles of the early twentieth century, was pretty much forgotten over the next thirty years. Then, as America looked back to the home and to homemade things, back to nature, and back to the comfortable ways of simpler days, wicker was discovered once again.

French chaise-recliner, popular on the Riviera in the 1920s and 1930s. Courtesy Cooper-Hewitt Museum, New York.

WICKER REVIVAL

Ruby Ross Wood was the most sought-after decorator of the 1930s. She had been the "doyenne" of the first *great* decorating department, at Wanamaker's in New York, and had gained further renown by writing articles on decorating for *Vogue* and *House & Garden.* She did the homes of Conde Nast, Edna Woolman Chase, Carmel Snow, and Greta Garbo, among many, many others. Such was her success that she found it necessary to hire an assistant, a young man just out of Princeton. His name was Billy Baldwin, and it wasn't many months before his talent became quite apparent. After one summer on the job he was allowed to work on his own, decorating for the fashionable people who flocked to the firm. Ina Claire, Cole Porter, Kitty Miller, and Diana Vreeland were favored ones he calls "stars in my crown."

Baldwin's approach was fresh, young, lively. Rooms through the 1930s and 1940s were stiff and formal and deadly pale. He took those rooms and enlivened them with color and light, gave them spirit and personality with printed fabrics and very comfortable furniture. In the 1950s he continued to make news as a style innovator. He used bright-colored cotton slipcovers on sofas and chairs, put simple shutters at windows, and added wicker.

No one had thought of wicker seriously for years and years until Billy Baldwin decided he had to have it. He had his own ideas about the way he wanted it to look: straight and modern in line, elegant enough to replace eighteenth-century furniture in drawing rooms. And late in the 1950s he asked the wicker crafting firm of Bielecky to translate his ideas into willow furniture. They were not revolutionary styles, but they were not meant to be. Baldwin explains:

> The inspiration came from a wonderful raffia-wrapped chair by the great decorator and furniture designer, Jean Michel Frank. I developed a bookcase with a frame of thick square lengths of wood wrapped with strips of willow and inset shelves of Formica-topped wood. I liked the bookcases so much that I adapted the idea for tables and benches that resembled the famous Parsons table with legs and aprons of wrapped willow and tops of any suitable material. (*Billy Baldwin Decorates*, New York: Holt, Rinehart & Winston, 1972)

The willow-wrapped Parsons styles, considered classics in furniture design today, were practical, functional, and timely—"in" in the contemporary taste. Other decorators ordered Baldwin's designs with enthusiasm, and Bielecky Brothers expanded the collection to include sofas and chairs. Wicker was on its way back to being chic.

Baldwin has been much copied, in decorating and in wicker ideas, but the success of his wicker owes much to his easy partnership with Bielecky, whose expertise brought Baldwin's designs brilliantly into being.

The Bielecky family had a long history of devotion to handcrafted wicker. In Poland the family had been renowned for its wicker craftsmanship. When Conrad and Andrew Bielecki came to America at the turn of the century, they set up a small shop and started weaving willow chairs. Their first style was a basket design of openwork stick wicker with curved back and braid trim. The brothers took orders from around the neighborhood and sold the chair for about one dollar and fifty cents. The wicker was comfortable, well made, and very inexpensive, and soon the Bieleckis offered two more styles to customers, and hired five Polish weavers to help production. In ten

The Bielecki brothers and the wicker craftsmen
they employed in front of their workshop in New York City
in 1902 with their early styles of basket chairs.
Courtesy Bielecky Brothers, New York.

Jennifer chair by Michael Taylor for Wicker, Wicker, Wicker.
Designed especially for Mrs. Norton Simon, who owns four
of them plus the matching ottomans. Upholstery is white
canvas duck, a signature of Michael Taylor, along with oversized square and round "basketball" pillows.
W. 66"; D. 54". Photograph: Charles Husted, San Francisco.

years of business they changed the spelling of the family name to Bielecky, upped the price of basket chairs to three dollars and fifty cents, and added dozens of new wicker styles to the line. By the 1920s Bielecky Brothers had an excellent reputation around New York for custom design and superb workmanship. Their good name and a newly initiated policy of allowing decorators to change, modify, or even originate wicker styles enabled the company to survive the next thirty years, years when wicker was out of fashion. A decorator can still choose any design from an old Bielecky catalogue and have it woven with whatever changes or modifications he wishes. As for prices, the original basket chair style costs over eight hundred dollars now. It is, of course, generously proportioned, beautifully made, meticulously upholstered, infinitely comfortable, and guaranteed to last, well, almost forever.

Today the Bieleckys as a family have the distinction of owning and operating the oldest continuous wicker business in this country. (Most other wicker is made in the Far East, the Philippines, Haiti, and Italy.) In their factory on Long Island there is an international group of eighteen weavers who make by hand the wicker furniture that is sent to clients all over the world. The company is still run by two brothers, third-generation Bieleckys, with Thomas Mennett, an in-house designer who has guided the styling for over twenty-five years.

While Billy Baldwin was working on the East Coast with new wicker looks and a simple, uncluttered approach to interiors, a young San Francisco designer, Michael Taylor, was giving rooms a clean, open-air-living quality with wicker and white-on-white-on-white.

Sparkling white interiors looked spanking new to a lot of Americans, although they had been a trademark of Syrie Maugham, the English decorator who was very

The skirted table designed by Michael Taylor for Wicker, Wicker, Wicker comes in two sizes: H. 31½" x Diam. 37½"; and H. 29½" x Diam. 30". H. of four-panel wicker screen: 96". Photograph: Charles Husted, San Francisco.

Square-back lounge chair and ottoman designed by Peter Rocchia is woven in Italy of a large-diameter reed. Sturdy and masculine, this trend-setting design heralded the overscaled look in wicker and the big braid trim. Chair: H. 29″; W. 30″; D. 32″. Ottoman: H. 17″; W. 30″; D. 25″. Courtesy Wickerworks, San Francisco.

Wave chaise by Danny Ho Fong. In the permanent collection of The Museum of Modern Art, New York. Steel frame wrapped with rattan. H. 17″; W. 82″; D. 24″. Courtesy Tropi-Cal, Los Angeles.

fashionable in this country in the 1920s and whose designs attracted great attention. But it wasn't just all that white that made such a decorating impact. It was Taylor's easy, breezy, back-to-nature feeling. The sun always seemed to shine in his rooms.

Taylor started with this approach in the 1950s; he's still with it today because he believes that people need natural things. He brings this idea home by using bamboo blinds instead of heavy curtains, straw matting instead of carpeting, plants all around, and plenty of wicker furniture, most of which he has designed. He designs no room without some wicker furniture, and he flatly states, "Add wicker to a room, and you add life."

His wicker is a definite decorating force: the lines are straight and pure; the styles, handsome and substantial. Somehow, though, the look is always light, even when the pieces are big. Taylor designed a chair for Jennifer Jones that is 66 inches wide by 54 inches deep; but it's not the size that impresses you, it's the perfect, simple elegance of the piece. His art has its imitators, but he still manages to be the one decorator whose interiors are so carefully composed and, at the same time, so earthy and inviting.

Taylor and Baldwin were ahead of the times; and after twenty years their designs still look fresh. They revived wicker as a material for furniture. They and a host of others—Peter Rocchia, Danny Ho Fong, John and Elinor McGuire, Waldo Fernandez—have given it its newest looks. But it was America's renewed interest in handcrafted things that brought back the old wicker looks as well.

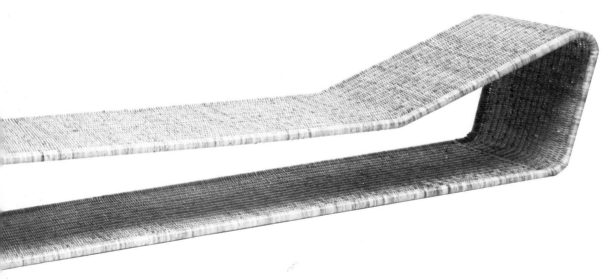

Horizon by Danny Ho Fong. Dining chair,
steel-pipe frame wrapped with core rattan.
The legs are satin stainless steel. H. 27";
W. 22"; D. 27". H. of seat: 18'; H. of arm: 27".
Courtesy Tropi-Cal, Los Angeles.

Butterfly chair, rattan with rawhide lacings to wrap
joints—a McGuire invention for strengthening their
furniture. H. 35¾''; W. 32½''; D. 21''. The McGuires
won the 1976 Pace Setter Award for their unique
furniture designs. In *Please Be Seated, The Evolution of
the Chair* (1970), Marvin D. Schwartz wrote that the
McGuire Company "raises wicker to high style and
suggests new shapes for the plastics engineers to
ponder." Courtesy the McGuire Co., San Francisco.

Generously oversized, with flaring
arms and deep cushion, this
armchair, woven of large-core cane,
was designed by Waldo Fernandez.
H. 28"; W. 44"; D. 44". Courtesy
Waldo Fernandez, Los Angeles.

This is a grouping of *Conchìglia divani* or
shell sofas, handmade by the firm of Vivai del
Sud in Rome exclusively for export to the
United States. H. 60″; W. 67″; D. 50″.
Courtesy Casa Bella Imports, Miami.

Mrs. Henry ("Sister") Parish II was the first decorator to use handcrafts to bring a homey quality to the rooms of her well-known clientele. She created personal, cozy, joyful places that oozed comfort and a happy peace of mind. She did it with lacquered brown-wrapping-paper walls, handwoven rugs, crocheted afghans, African-inspired fabrics, American Indian and early American decorative arts, baskets, colored ceilings, hand-stenciled floors, and old-fashioned wicker furniture. She put quilts on walls, homemade decoupage shades on lamps, and miniature gardens in baskets on porches. She set old-fashioned wicker chairs around kitchen tables, turned wicker trunks into bedside tables, and repainted sets of old backyard wicker for summer living rooms.

The love for wicker grew with her from childhood. "I think everyone must have a first memory of some house, some room, a vivid picture that will remain deep down in one forever." This is her description of her own memory:

> White walls, pale yellow matting on the floor, and wicker furniture painted white. The material of the cushions and curtains was a heavy white cotton printed with vines and roses. The mantel, also white, had a deep organdy-and-lace ruffle tacked onto the edge of the shelf. A gold clock stood under a glass dome; on each side of it were white candlesticks with angels clustered at their bases. There were white wicker tables too, some covered in lace to the floor, and a tea tray on a white wicker two-wheeled cart, with matching roses-and-vines material shirred underneath the glass top. There were bowls of flowers, filled every day with roses from the garden, and family pictures in silver frames . . .(Katharine Tweed, ed., *The Finest Rooms by America's Great Decorators*, New York: The Viking Press, 1964)

When Mrs. Parish decorated her first house, her own, in 1928, she created another favorite room: "Off the living room we built a small greenhouse with an old brick floor. We furnished it with a huge sofa covered with yellow and dozens of pillows. A skirted table displayed a collection of personal treasures. Here two wicker chairs crept back into my life. This is where we really lived . . . "

She does understand how people really live, or how they really should like to; and making rooms that reflect that special perception is her special talent. Her emphasis is on pleasure and contentment, and she is famous for her natural, comfortable, "undecorated" look. There is no one who does it better.

A good copy of a Heywood-Wakefield loveseat from a turn-of-the-century catalogue. H. 21½"; W. 47"; D. 20". By Elaine Cohen for Design Institute of America, New York.

Natural and comfortable, that's what people want to be and what they want their homes to be. The emphasis in decorating today is the same as the emphasis in living. People are creating their own personal spaces that reflect their individuality, choosing furniture that is an invitation to relax, using lighting to purpose, displaying the things they love, putting plants everywhere, and weaving in wicker, old or new. There's wicker in grand rooms and in humble ones, in cozy rooms or starkly modern ones. It may be just one piece—a peacock chair or a 1920s chaise or a curvy, curly Victorian rocker; or even less—maybe just a basket for the *Ficus benjamina*; or lots more—Italian wicker sofas, basket chairs, and hassocks creating a comfortable mood in a living room that also includes two Louis XV armchairs, kilim rugs, a grand piano, and an oriental palm.

Michael Taylor explained to this writer the decoration of his own house in California as follows:

I'd rather look at a plant than a bad pair of curtains or a fake anything. If you're going to buy an expensive piece of sculpture, you're spending a lot of money. But you can just get a plant and enjoy it and have something beautiful. I'm an incurable romantic. I learned long ago that nature can be a decorator's best friend, and she's mine. Bedsides plants, I have a bed made of alder trees, bedside tables of cedar stumps with marble tops, and floors paved with Yosemite slate laid like flagging. The wicker furniture I have is organic and from nature, too. What nature hasn't contributed man has: a Chinese bronze deer, ancient Chinese screens, a William and Mary table with balloon legs . . .

The mix is prophetic: modern decor is truly eclectic. No hard-and-fast rules dictate what's right for rooms any longer. Now decorating becomes the individual. Pillow furniture in cotton duck clusters around an antique lacquered chest. An 1880s bentwood highchair makes a 1970s plant stand. Quilts are treated like tapestries; Sarouk rugs are spread on beds. Wicker baskets are hung as graphics. Wicker-and-chrome chairs surround chrome-and-glass dining tables as well as old oak ones. Wicker sofas add equal parts of pleasure to settings they may share with a Coromandel screen, a Quaker chest, a handwoven dhurrie rug.

Wicker. Its form has changed over time, but its audience hasn't. Wicker is homey— simply, practically, naturally, comfortably homey—and that appeals to everyone.

An interesting copy of a Mission wicker chair.
H. 44″; W. 22″; D. 28″. By Elaine Cohen for Design Institute
of America, New York.

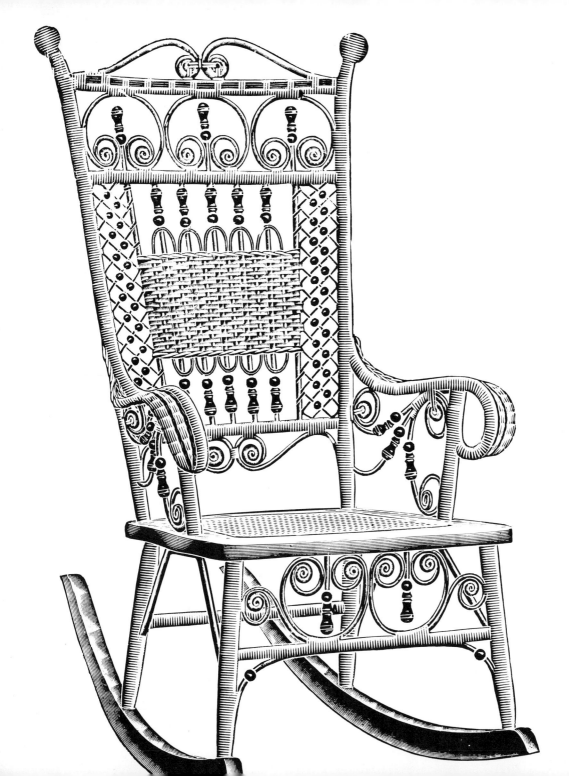

INDEX

PATRICIA CORBIN is a free-lance writer who contributes articles on design and decorating to *The New York Times*. She has been both an editor and a columnist at *House & Garden* magazine. Currently, she is planning a television program on design-related life-styles.